MAYA LIN

ASIAN AMERICANS OF ACHIEVEMENT

Margaret Cho

Daniel Inouye

Michelle Kwan

Bruce Lee

Maya Lin

Yo-Yo Ma

Isamu Noguchi

Amy Tan

Vera Wang

Kristi Yamaguchi

ASIAN AMERICANS OF ACHIEVEMENT

MAYA LIN

TOM LASHNITS

CHELSEA HOUSE
PUBLISHERS
An imprint of Infobase Publishing

Maya Lin

Chelsea House
An imprint of Infobase Publishing
132 West 31st Street
New York, NY 10001

ISBN-10: 0-7910-9268-2
ISBN-13: 978-0-7910-9268-2

Library of Congress Cataloging-in-Publication Data
Lashnits, Tom.
    Maya Lin / Tom Lashnits.
       p. cm. — (Asian Americans of achievement)
    Includes bibliographical references and index.
    ISBN 0-7910-9268-2 (hardcover)
    1. Lin, Maya Ying—Juvenile literature. 2. Chinese American architects—
       Biography—Juvenile literature. 3. Vietnam Veterans Memorial (Washington, D.C.)—
       Juvenile literature. I. Title. II. Series.
    NA737.L48L37 2007
    720.92—dc22
    [B]
    2006026064   08384

Chelsea House books are available at special discounts when purchased in
bulk quantities for businesses, associations, institutions, or sales promotions.
Please call our Special Sales Department in New York at (212) 967-8800
or (800) 322-8755.

You can find Chelsea House on the World Wide Web at http://www.chelseahouse.com

Series design by Erika K. Arroyo
Cover design by Ben Peterson

Printed in the United States of America

Bang FOF 10 9 8 7 6 5 4 3 2 1   .

This book is printed on acid-free paper.

All links and Web addresses were checked and verified to be correct at the time of
publication. Because of the dynamic nature of the Web, some addresses and links may
have changed since publication and may no longer be valid.

CONTENTS

A Date
With Destiny

Maya Lin was beginning her senior year at Yale University in New Haven, Connecticut. She was short and slight, weighing less than a hundred pounds. As a mark of individuality, she let her long black hair hang halfway down her back. She had always been known as the smart girl in the class. She also had a strong sense of herself and her impressive capabilities.

That year she was taking a class on funerary architecture—a course put together by a group of art students who wanted to study buildings and sculptures memorializing people who have died. For one assignment, the professor, Andrus Burr, asked the young artists to imagine there was a World War III—then design a memorial for its victims. Maya Lin came up with what she described as "a tomblike underground structure that I deliberately made to be a very futile and frustrating experience."

Professor Burr was disappointed in her work. It was depressing, he said. If he had a brother who'd died in World

7

War III, he would not want to visit Lin's memorial. It looked too much like a tomb.

"I was somewhat puzzled," Lin explained. "He didn't quite understand that World War III would be of such devastation that none of us would be around to visit any memorial, and that my design was a prewar commentary. In asking myself what a memorial to a third world war would be, I came up with a political statement that was meant as a deterrent."

Lin was an independent thinker. She knew what she wanted to say and didn't care much what other people thought. She had always gone her own way.

Maya Lin came from a typical American town, the college town of Athens, Ohio. Her childhood was anything but typical, however. She was the daughter of Chinese immigrants. Her parents had fled the Communists in China, long before Maya was born. They found a life for themselves as professors at Ohio University, a relatively small state school located among the hills in southeastern Ohio.

Growing up, Maya was the only person of Asian descent in her class. She was a loner; she hung out with her family and entertained herself by reading books, exploring the woods around her house, and playing in her room. In high school, Maya won honors as a top student in both math and science. She was also interested in the arts, however. She liked making things with her hands, just like her father, who spent many hours in his studio on the Ohio University campus, fashioning pottery and ceramic pieces.

When Maya Lin arrived at Yale, she continued to study math and science. She also found herself gravitating toward courses in art, architecture, and sculpture. In her junior year, Lin decided to major in architecture, and she spent a semester studying in Demark, Germany, France, and Greece.

In the fall of 1980, one of the students in Lin's funerary class saw a notice posted on a bulletin board at the school. The poster announced a nationwide competition, which was open

Maya Lin was a 21-year-old Yale University architecture student when she won $20,000 for her design of the Vietnam Veterans Memorial.

to anyone, to design a memorial for the veterans of the Vietnam War. It would be erected on the Mall in Washington, D.C., and would commemorate the 58,000 Americans who died fighting in Southeast Asia in the 1960s and early 1970s. The young artists in Professor Burr's seminar decided this competition would make a great final project for their class.

There were certain specifications for the memorial. It was supposed to include the names of the soldiers who died in the war. It should fit in with the environment. Above all, according to the sponsors, the monument should rise above politics, allowing future visitors to remember and honor the people who gave their lives, whether those visitors supported the war or opposed it bitterly.

Maya Lin didn't know much about the Vietnam War. When the war was being fought, she was a child, studying and playing in the yard. She didn't really read the newspaper or watch the news on TV. She never went to an antiwar demonstration.

Now, thinking about the memorial, she decided it would be counterproductive to launch into a huge research project on Vietnam and all the controversy over the war. "I felt that the politics had eclipsed the veterans, their service, and their lives," she remembered in her autobiography, *Boundaries*. "I wanted to create a memorial that everyone would be able to respond to, regardless of whether one thought our country should or should not have participated in the war."

So instead, Lin continued researching monuments that commemorated historic wars and fallen heroes. She was particularly taken with memorials for World War I. She felt that they were the first to acknowledge the sacrifice made by individual soldiers. She explained:

Many of these memorials included the names of those killed. Partly it was a practical need to list those whose bodies could not be identified—since dog tags as identification had not been adopted and, due to the nature of the warfare, many killed were not identifiable—but I think as well the listing of names reflected a response by these designers to the horrors of World War I, to the immense loss of life.

Lin reviewed her research and thought about what she wanted to incorporate in the assignment: the names of the fallen, the hope for reconciliation, and the harmony with the environment. She then set off for Washington, D.C., to see for herself the place where the memorial would be erected.

She met with a couple of her friends after Thanksgiving vacation and walked around the Mall, the grassy park that runs from the U.S. Capitol building to the Potomac River. The Mall already contained two of the most famous memorials in the world—the Washington Monument and the Lincoln Memorial. Now it would also be home to the Vietnam Veterans Memorial.

On that sunny, crisp November day, Lin saw the park in all its beauty. Some people were playing Frisbee. As she gazed across the fields, she recalled, "It just popped into my head." She envisioned the design of the memorial instantly:

> When I looked at the site I just knew I wanted something horizontal that took you in, that made you feel safe within that park, yet at the same time reminding you of the dead. So I just imagined opening up the earth. . . . It's like opening up your hands. You're using the earth, asking people to come in, protecting people from the sounds of the city and in a way that's no more threatening than two open hands.

Maya Lin and her friends spent several hours on the Mall, exploring the area, taking in the views. They photographed the site and made some sketches. "I imagined taking a knife and cutting into the earth, opening it up, an initial violence and pain that in time would heal," she explained. "The grass would grow back, but the initial cut would remain a pure flat surface in the earth with a polished, mirrored surface, much like the surface on a geode when you cut it and polish the edge. The names . . . would become the memorial; there was no need to embellish the design further. The people and their names would allow everyone to respond and remember."

Excited by her idea, Lin returned to college in New Haven and found herself in the cafeteria making a model of her memorial in the mashed potatoes. She spent a couple of weeks sketching her design and then making a proper clay model.

Lin envisioned the edge of her monument, the horizontal wall. It had to be made from polished black granite, because she knew it would reflect the faces of the people reading the names. She decided there would actually be two walls, and they would meet at an angle. One of the walls would point to the Lincoln Memorial, the other to the Washington Monument.

She submitted her work to the class, as did the other students, and they all discussed the various designs. The professor weighed in. He liked Maya Lin's idea.

Some students tried to persuade Lin to change the color of the stone from black to white. They thought white would be a more suitable color for a memorial and it would match other memorials on the Mall. Maya Lin resisted, however. The wall had to be black, she said.

Then they decided that the listing of the names on the wall should be in chronological order, rather than alphabetical order. Listing the people in the order in which they died would give the monument a clear sense of history. Friends and relatives who visited the monument would locate the names of their loved ones in the context of the time span of the war.

The competition called for participants to send in drawings of their sculpture, along with a short essay describing their work. Lin had some simple pastel sketches of her concept, but she had trouble writing the essay. Like a lot of college students,

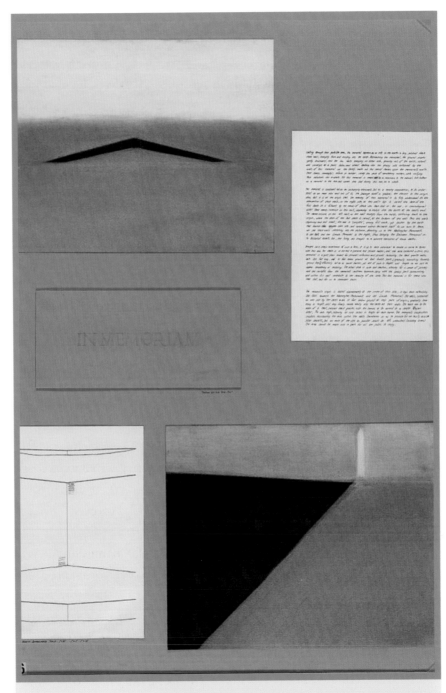

The simplicity and power of Maya Lin's competition drawing for the Vietnam Veterans Memorial stood out from the other designs submitted.

she found herself stalling and procrastinating, until March arrived and the deadline loomed.

"I kept reworking and reediting the final description," she later explained. "I actually never quite finished it. I ended up at the last minute writing freehand directly onto the presentation boards (you can see a few misprints on the actual page), and then I sent the project in, never expecting to hear about it again."

Lin didn't have a car, so a friend drove her to the post office. She mailed her submission to Washington, D.C. She was the only student from the class who actually sent in a design.

2

How the Memorial Got Started

Little did this diminutive college student know that when she dropped off her package at the post office, she would set in motion a force that would change her life. It would also embroil her in a national controversy that would affect millions of Americans across the country.

The Vietnam Veterans Memorial was a project about to explode. It all began with a common American soldier, a Vietnam War veteran himself, a man named Jan Scruggs. Scruggs grew up in Maryland; he was the son of a milkman and a waitress. When he graduated from high school, Scruggs didn't know what he wanted to do with his life. Instead of applying to college, like most of his friends, he decided to go into the army. In 1969, when he was 19 years old, Scruggs was sent to Vietnam. He carried a rifle as an infantryman. Soon he was skulking through the jungle, fighting the heat, the exhaustion, and the Communist guerrillas.

Scruggs spent one terror-filled night pinned down by an enemy machine gun, escaping only after an American soldier

U.S. Marines blow up bunkers and tunnels used by the Vietcong in May 1966, during the Vietnam War.

exposed his own position, to draw enemy fire. The man was shot to death, but his heroic act gave his comrades, including Jan Scruggs, the few precious moments they needed to retreat.

In the year Scruggs was on duty in Vietnam, he saw more than half of his squad either killed or wounded, until he too was hit with enemy shrapnel and finally sent home as a decorated veteran. Back in Maryland, Scruggs didn't know what to do. There was no homecoming parade or public ceremony to thank him for his service. Instead, he saw indifference, and even

BRIEF HISTORY OF THE VIETNAM WAR

Vietnam: It was the longest war in U.S. history. The very name conjures up controversy.

The United States was drawn into the conflict in Southeast Asia in the 1950s, after France lost colonial control over the area. When the French left, Vietnam was divided into the Communist North and the Nationalist South. Elections were supposed to be held to unify the country, but instead the South declared itself an independent nation.

Consequently, the Communists in the south, called the Vietcong, began a guerrilla war against the government. They attacked South Vietnam installations, then disappeared into the jungle. The North Vietnamese supported the Vietcong, in an effort to unify the country under the Communist flag.

The United States, fearing a Communist takeover, came to the aid of South Vietnam. By 1963, a handful of military advisors had been sent to Vietnam. In 1965, President Lyndon Johnson stepped up the American commitment by sending in combat troops.

Many Americans supported military involvement in Vietnam, believing the United States was fighting for democracy. Others, however, felt that America had no business sending troops to wage someone else's war and to prop up what they believed was a corrupt South Vietnamese government.

As American soldiers began to die in ever-increasing numbers, opposition to the war became more strident. Americans took to the streets to protest the war, and young people fled to Canada or Sweden to avoid the military draft. In 1968, facing increasing opposition because of the war, Johnson announced that he would not run for reelection as president. After an acrimonious campaign, Richard Nixon, who claimed to have a secret plan to end the war, won the presidency, and for the next several years he fought for "peace with honor."

(continues)

(continued)

Finally in 1973, Secretary of State Henry Kissinger cobbled together a peace plan, and the majority of American troops came home. South Vietnam was left to fend for itself, and it soon failed. In April 1975, the Communists completed their takeover, and the last of the Americans fled for their lives by clambering aboard helicopters.

In all, about 58,000 Americans died in the war. The average age of the men killed in Vietnam was only 19 years old. A sorry chapter in American history was finally over—but as the building of the Vietnam Veterans Memorial proved, the controversy would not soon be forgotten.

hostility, from people who asked why he was stupid enough to go to Vietnam, or why he was killing poor innocent civilians 10,000 miles (16,100 kilometers) from home.

Scruggs took a job as a security guard. Then he quit and traveled around the country for a while. He enrolled in a community college, then transferred to American University in Washington, D.C. He eventually earned a master's degree in counseling and went to work for the U.S. Department of Labor.

The public's lack of respect and recognition for Vietnam veterans continued to haunt him, though, even after the last Americans came home when the war ended in 1975. In his autobiography, *To Heal a Nation,* Scruggs wrote that he could not leave behind the memory of his days in Vietnam, of the men who never returned.

One day in March 1979, Scruggs saw *The Deer Hunter,* an award-winning film starring Robert DeNiro, Christopher Walken, and Meryl Streep. The movie told the story of a group of friends from Pennsylvania and showed the impact the Vietnam

War had on their lives. Scruggs went home that evening, and he couldn't sleep. He spent an agonizing night experiencing flashbacks of combat in Vietnam. By morning, he had made a decision. "I'm going to build a memorial to all the guys who served in Vietnam," he told his wife resolutely. "It'll have the name of everyone killed."

Scruggs met with other veterans and held a press conference in Washington, D.C. He began to raise money. He recruited volunteers, and they filed the necessary papers to form a nonprofit organization they called the Vietnam Veterans Memorial Fund (VVMF). This small group of vets agreed on their objectives. They would obtain land for the memorial in 1980 and focus on raising the money in 1981. Then, they would construct the memorial, and dedicate it on Veterans Day in 1982.

These vets also agreed that they would resist the temptation to express their own personal views about the Vietnam War— whether they had supported it or opposed it, why they thought the war had been lost. There were too many differing opinions on the Vietnam War still circulating, and the vets wanted the memorial to include everyone. They resolved that the memorial would be strictly nonpolitical and focus on honoring the patriotism and the sacrifice of the soldiers who served.

Robert W. Doubek, a Washington lawyer, became a key activist for VVMF. He told a congressional committee in October 1979, "Over 2.7 million Americans served in Vietnam. More than 57,000 died, and over 300,000 were wounded. . . . The Vietnam Veterans Memorial is conceived as a means to promote the healing and reconciliation of the country after the divisions caused by war. . . . It will symbolize the experience of the Vietnam generation for the generations which follow."

Volunteers began lobbying Congress, asking for a location on the Mall where they could construct the memorial. Congress would not have to appropriate any money. The veterans said they would pay for the memorial through contributions from the public. But they did need the land. They would also need approvals from various commissions and government agencies.

Jan Scruggs, Robert Doubek, and their fellow volunteers asked for two acres between the Lincoln Memorial and the Washington Monument, in an area known as Constitution Gardens, located just off Constitution Avenue near one of the reflecting pools on the Mall. They persuaded Senator Charles Mathias from Maryland to introduce the bill. A number of co-sponsors represented all sides of the political spectrum. Supporters included both Senator Barry Goldwater, who had run for president in 1964 as a tough-talking, pro-war hawk, and Senator George McGovern, who ran for president in 1972 as a dove who wanted the United States to get out of Vietnam. Each of them understood the idea that the Vietnam veterans could be honored, regardless of the politics of the war.

After several months of intense lobbying, the U.S. Senate unanimously passed a bill authorizing the use of this land for the memorial. After more politicking, the U.S. House of Representatives went along with the idea.

Once the land was approved and the fundraising under way, the VVMF had to decide just what sort of memorial would be appropriate to commemorate the Vietnam veterans. Right from the beginning, Scruggs wanted the names of the dead soldiers inscribed on the memorial. Everyone agreed on that. What else could it be, though? What would it look like? Who would design it?

Washington sculptor Frederick Hart, who knew some of the veterans, offered to design the memorial. He came up with some ideas that he showed the VVMF, but the veterans demurred. Rather than decide on something themselves, they agreed to open up the process to the public. At first, they thought they could ask several top architectural firms to submit designs, and they would pick the one they liked best. Then, they reconsidered. What did they know about art or design? How would they know they picked the right one?

Members of the military police restrain Vietnam War protesters during a sit-in at the Pentagon in 1967.

Finally, the veterans decided to hold a public competition. Why not give every American the chance to offer a design for the memorial? Wasn't that the democratic way? Besides, it wouldn't be the first time a famous Washington building was created as the result of a design competition. Both the White House, in the 1790s, and the Washington Monument, in the 1830s, came into existence that way.

The VVMF also decided, rather than choosing the winner themselves, they would assemble a panel of experts to select the very best of all the entries. Scruggs and his colleagues gathered together a jury of eight nationally recognized experts: two architects, two landscape architects, three sculptors, and one art critic. This blue-ribbon panel would review all the entries and pick the winner—although it would still be up to the veterans to accept the verdict.

The experts were asked to ignore any political agenda and to rise above any specific style of art. The judges should select a design that "best honors the memory of those Americans who died by serving our country in Vietnam, the memory of those who were wounded, and the memory of those who served." The memorial, according to the veterans, should be "reflective and contemplative in character ... neither too commanding nor too deferential."

In November 1980, the VVMF announced the competition to the media, the public, and the entire world. Consequently, as word went out, that fateful notice appeared on the bulletin board at Yale University.

The cost of the contest, including a $20,000 prize, would be paid out of contributions that were already coming in. The largest by far was a $160,000 gift from Texas billionaire Ross Perot, a graduate of the U.S. Naval Academy.

The names of the jurors were announced. The reaction was uniformly positive. The presence of the distinguished judges was an honor to the veterans and only added authority and prestige to the whole idea of a memorial.

3

And
the Winner Is . . .

Entries to the VVMF design competition began to come in, arriving in Washington in a trickle during January 1981, then by the hundreds in February. By the time the deadline rolled around, on March 31, 1981, the fund had received a total of 1,421 submissions.

One of the Vietnam vets, who was assistant secretary of the Air Force, arranged for all the entries to be shipped to a gigantic airplane hangar at Andrews Air Force Base, outside Washington, D.C. The submissions were unpacked and set out on display for the jury to examine. The contestants had been instructed to put their name inside an envelope and tape it to the back of their submission. The judging would be blind. Although the names of the artists were kept secret, it was clear that many of the designs were submitted by professional architects, established artists, and reputable design firms.

By the last week of April, the jury was ready to deliberate. The experts met to elect a chairperson, and they reviewed the criteria set forth by the VVMF. Then the eight judges proceeded to spread out and examine the display boards. The proposals came in all shapes and sizes. Some were traditional designs, featuring columns, obelisks, or towers to mark the historic gravity of the war. Others were more creative: a sculptured helicopter pad, an outsized army helmet, a huge pair of GI boots, and a big peace sign.

The judges quickly rejected concepts that were too heroic or overtly partisan, as well as those imitating the classical memorials already dotting the Washington landscape. Instead, they gravitated toward the modern, abstract designs that seemed more in tune with the complexities of modern war.

In *To Heal a Nation*, Jan Scruggs and cowriter Joel Swerdlow recounted how that very first evening one juror bumped into a friend at a Washington hotel.

The friend asked the juror, "What's the quality of the entries?"

"About what you'd expect," came the answer.

"How's it going?"

"Very strange. One keeps haunting me."

After a day or so of deliberations, the judges had eliminated almost 1,200 submissions. A little more than 200 survived the first cut.

"That evening," Scruggs and Swerdlow went on, "the juror once again saw his friend. The juror shook his head. 'It's still haunting me,' he said."

That entry was one of the last to come in—No. 1,026. The soft pastel drawings were not as sophisticated as some of the competitors, yet they exhibited a quiet but unmistakable strength. "There's no escape from its power," said one judge. Another expert commented that it "looks back to death and forward to life," while still another mused that it's "not a thing of joy, but a large space for hope."

No one knew who had sent in entry No. 1,026, the one that was so captivating the judges. The competition was anonymous; the names were hidden.

Two days later, the judges narrowed down the field to 39 submissions. They decided they would recognize 15 designs by placing them on an honorable mention list. Then they would pick a third-place finisher, a runner-up, and the winner.

The panel pondered some more and discussed the merits of the finalists. Finally, the chairperson of the jury took a poll. The outcome was unanimous. The winner was No. 1,026. The jury voted a second time, just to make sure. Again, the result was unanimous.

The next day, the judges presented their decision to a group from the VVMF. Jan Scruggs was there with his fellow volunteers,

Maya Lin presents the model of the Vietnam memorial she designed in 1981 in Washington D.C.

including Jack Wheeler and Robert Doubek. One of the judges went behind a curtain and brought out the third-place finisher, which would receive a $5,000 award. It was a submission from an Alexandria, Virginia, landscape architectural firm, featuring a figure by Frederick Hart, the sculptor who was familiar to the group of veterans. Second place went to a professional firm from New York that had fashioned an imposing abstract design of twisted metal and marble pillars.

Then the ultimate moment arrived. The jury brought out the winner, the one selected above all others for the Vietnam Memorial. The poster showed simple pastel drawings of a huge black *V* cut sideways into the ground. The judges explained to the veterans that this entry fulfilled all the requirements of the competition, in a simple yet profound way. "Of all the proposals submitted," they said, "this most clearly meets the spirit and formal requirements of the program. It is contemplative and reflective. It is superbly harmonious with its site and yet frees the visitors from the noise and traffic of the surrounding city."

The judges continued, "It is uniquely horizontal, entering the earth rather than piercing the sky. This is very much a memorial of our own times, one that could not have been achieved in another time or place." Jan Scruggs was bewildered, however. He thought there must be some mistake. Had a third grader entered the contest and somehow won?

The group of veterans sat in silence. What was this thing anyway? A bird? A huge black bat? Or possibly a boomerang—perhaps symbolizing how Vietnam had come back to haunt the country? It was hard to visualize from this drawing what the final project would look like, with its two big walls, each one more than 200 feet (61 meters) long, cut into the ground. Silence hung heavy in the vast airplane hangar.

Then Jan Scruggs saw the names—the wall that inscribed the names of all the soldiers who had died in Vietnam. That's exactly what he had envisioned right from the beginning. Here it was—the wall of names that would live on forever on the

Mall. It was fellow veteran Jack Wheeler who broke the silence. "This is a work of genius," he declared simply and solemnly.

Robert Doubek recalled, "When we had understood, when the genius of this simple concept took its effect on us, we embraced and congratulated one another. We were thrilled."

Along with the drawings came the essay explaining the design: "Walking through this parklike area, the memorial appears as a rift in the earth—a long, polished black stone wall, emerging from and receding into the earth. . . ."

The design did not mention the country of Vietnam, nor the war itself—only the names. The names would be engraved into the walls of the V, in chronological rather than alphabetical order. Lin explained, "These names, seemingly infinite in number, convey the sense of overwhelming numbers, while unifying those individuals into a whole. For this memorial is not meant as a memorial to the individual, but rather as a memorial to the men and women who died during the war, a whole."

The judges went on to explain to the veterans, "This memorial with its wall of names becomes a place of quiet reflection and a tribute to those who served their nation in difficult times. . . . The designer has created an eloquent place where the simple setting of earth, sky, and remembered names contains messages for all who will know this place."

The chairman of the jury added, "Great art is a complex matter. All great works furnish material for endless debate. We are certain this will be debated for years to come. This is healthy and ought to be expected."

Robert Doubek looked up entry No. 1,026. Everyone had expected that the winner would be a well-known professional, probably associated with a respectable architectural firm in Washington or New York. Instead, the name read: Maya Ying Lin. The address and phone number indicated she was from New Haven, Connecticut.

Maya Lin never dreamed her design would win. "I liked my idea, but I knew it was never going to be chosen—it was too different, too strange," she said. In fact, while she got A's in most of her classes at Yale, her Vietnam Veterans Memorial design had only earned her a B in the funerary course.

Now, though, on May 1, 1981, she was attending class at Yale when, as she recalled, "My roommate came and got me and said, 'Don't get your hopes up, but you got a call from Washington.'" They would call again in 15 minutes.

"I went running back to my room and waited for them to call back. 'Don't get your hopes up,' they said when they called back, 'but we want to talk with you about your design.'"

"I didn't quite understand," Maya Lin admitted. "So they told me again."

Still, Lin didn't know precisely why the representatives from the Vietnam Veterans Memorial Fund wanted to meet with her. Maybe they had some questions? Maybe she had won an honorable mention? She could only wait and see.

Three people from the VVMF flew up to New Haven. They met with the young artist in her dormitory room. That's when they confirmed that yes, she had indeed won a prize. . . . She had won first prize!

Lin showed little reaction to the news. Perhaps she didn't appreciate the significance of this decision. Later, she recalled that her first feeling was one of disbelief. Nevertheless, somewhat in a state of shock, she agreed to fly down to Washington to attend the announcement of the award. She called her parents in Ohio to tell them the news. She tried to sleep that night.

The next day, she boarded a plane and arrived in Washington to meet with the sponsors of the competition. When she walked into the room, the veterans gave her a round of applause. That's when it sunk in. She was the one.

Lin then had a couple of days to prepare herself for the announcement of the award to the public, and to rehearse what she was going to say at the press conference. She had a couple of days to prepare herself to become an instant celebrity.

Dozens of reporters and camera crews showed up for the unveiling at the American Institute of Architects. Robert Doubek pulled back a sheet covering the design, and Lin read her statement, explaining that the memorial would consist of two walls, each more than 200 feet (61 meters) long. They would meet at a shallow angle, with one wall stretching out toward the Washington Monument, the other pointing to the Lincoln Memorial, both of them merging with the earth.

The names would be inscribed in chronological order, beginning at the juncture of the two walls, according to the dates of the deaths. The first names, from 1959, would start at the right-hand wall and progress to the end. The names would pick up again at the end of the left-hand wall and continue back to the middle, ending in 1975. The last death would circle back to where the first name is engraved, closing this chapter in American history. "Thus the war's beginning and end meet; the war is 'complete,' coming full circle," as she wrote in her statement for the competition.

At first, the reaction to Lin's design was enthusiastic. The journalists at the unveiling applauded her presentation. Initial reviews in the newspapers were positive. The *New York Times* enthused, "Its extreme dignity and restraint honors these veterans with more poignancy, surely, than most more conventional monuments. . . . The design is 'minimalist,' but . . . the minimalism of the gifted artist able to use simple means to achieve a complex end."

Maya Lin's winning design was brought before the National Capital Planning Commission, which had to endorse the project, as well as the Commission of Fine Arts, which also had to give its stamp of approval. Both commissions signed off on the design itself, as well as the location between the Lincoln Memorial and the Washington Monument.

Meanwhile, Lin went back to college and finished up her senior year, graduating from Yale with a degree in architecture only a few weeks after winning the competition. Then she

Jan Scruggs *(left)* founder and president of the Vietnam Veterans Memorial Fund and Maya Lin *(right)* stand in front of an inscription bearing the names of military personnel killed or listed as missing in Vietnam, during a news conference on October 28, 1981, in Washington, D.C.

packed up her things, caught a ride to Washington, D.C., and moved into an apartment with some friends. Her new job was to help build the memorial.

As a newly minted college graduate, Lin did not have the skills or experience to develop the project by herself. So the VVMF contracted with a Washington architecture firm to actually construct the memorial. The firm, in turn, hired Lin as a design consultant. She would do all the things that apprentice architects do in their first job, learning the nuts and bolts of construction, while also being on hand to consult on the progress of the memorial.

The first issue was where to place the memorial on the two acres that Congress had turned over to the VVMF. The young designer, along with a landscape architect, spent hours crawling over Constitution Gardens, surveying the site on the ground and peering out from the top of the Washington Monument, searching for just the right spot. They not only had to consider the artistic elements of the site, but they also had to pay attention to such practical matters as drainage, slopes, and access.

Once, when they thought they had pinpointed the perfect place for the memorial, they marked out the location by driving stakes into the ground. The next morning, however, the stakes were gone. Not realizing the significance of the stakes, maintenance people from the National Park Service had pulled them out.

Lin again found the ideal location. This time she drove the stakes far enough into the ground so that the Park Service employees wouldn't see them. The trouble was, when she went back to the site, she couldn't find them, either. She went through the exercise once again, and this time when she knelt down to drive in a stake, she found one of the old ones. Then she knew. She had the right spot.

Lin worked with the architectural firm to iron out all the details of the project. They made sure to provide a sidewalk with wheelchair access and a safety curb. They discussed all the practical issues involved in carving the names into the wall. And the firm came up with a panel configuration where, in case of damage, a panel could be replaced. Given the divisions generated by the Vietnam War itself, it was not unreasonable to think that a group of protesters or terrorists might at some point try to target the memorial.

Just as initial support for the Vietnam War itself evaporated and then turned to confusion and anger, however, support for the Vietnam Veterans Memorial soon began to fracture. Perhaps, as Lin herself suggested, the conflict was inevitable. The memorial had to satisfy so many constituencies, the chances were remote that everyone would agree. The politicians had one vision. The old opponents of the Vietnam War had a different idea. The art community had yet another. Finally, of course, the veterans themselves couldn't all be expected to have the same view—they were as varied in their backgrounds and opinions as the American public at large.

So now, just as Americans had differing opinions about the war itself, they came to express differing opinions about the unusual design proposed for the memorial. Some veterans felt that the design was not very patriotic. They wondered, Why is the memorial being placed underground? Why does it have to be black? Shouldn't it be white?

The first to complain was Ross Perot, the billionaire (and future presidential candidate) who had donated $160,000 to hold the competition. He stoked the fires of discontent. Some veterans said the memorial looked like a wound in the earth; others called it a body count on the Mall.

In October 1981, almost six months after Maya Lin's design had been named the winner, the Fine Arts Commission held a meeting to hear the developing reactions to the design. Lin, a 21-year-old college graduate, was sitting in the audience.

One Vietnam veteran stood up and told the commission: "When I came home from Vietnam in December of 1968, I was literally spat upon in the Chicago airport as I walked through in my uniform. That spit hurt. It went through me like a spear. . . . When I saw the winning design I was truly stunned. I thought that the most insulting and demeaning memorial to our Vietnam experience that was possible."

The young designer sat stone-faced in the audience. She had tried to keep politics out of her design. She was an artist, not an expert on Vietnam. She had only been in grade school when this speaker was spat on in the Chicago airport.

The criticism from this veteran was just beginning, however. "One needs no artistic education to see this memorial design for what it is—a black scar," he charged. "Black. The universal color of sorrow and shame and degradation in all societies worldwide. In a hole. Hidden as though out of shame. As a Vietnam veteran who feels dishonored by this design, I call on the commission to reopen the competition and to require that the winning design be chosen by a jury composed exclusively of Vietnam veterans."

Soon opposition to the Memorial, and to Lin's design, was organized and became increasingly vocal. Several U.S. senators and government officials spoke out against Lin's concept. Ross Perot withdrew his name from the list of memorial sponsors. Some critics carped that Lin's design looked like a giant erosion control project. Others read into the V-shaped design a conspiracy to produce a giant peace sign. One conservative Washington think-tanker charged that one of the judges for the contest was a Communist.

Some critics got personal. Lin was a woman, they pointed out, when the vast majority of Vietnam vets were men. She was so young, while the vets were now pushing into middle age. How could a girl who knew nothing about the Vietnam War presume to speak for battle-hardened Vietnam vets?

There was one other mostly unspoken, but unfair, issue: This memorial, meant to commemorate American soldiers who died fighting against Asians, was created by a woman of Asian descent. The more the vets saw her image—in the newspapers, on TV, in

EUROPEAN INSPIRATION

Lin says she takes her artistic inspiration from the hills and the ancient Indian mounds she found in the woods around her house when she was growing up in Ohio. There undoubtedly is some Asian influence in her work, as well as a certain spare and simple approach that suggests Scandinavian design.

Scandinavian? Where did that come from? In her junior year as a Yale undergraduate, before she ever heard of the Vietnam Veterans Memorial, Lin spent a semester abroad. She enrolled at Copenhagen University in Denmark, taking courses in city planning and landscape design.

While in Copenhagen, Lin discovered an enormous cemetery, Assistens Kirkegaard. Hans Christian Andersen and other famous Danes are buried there. She liked the way the cemetery was integrated into the landscape, instead of being walled off from the city. She noted:

> As an architect, you're out to analyze what's going on. I started walking through the cemetery. Unlike in America, cemeteries [in Europe] are used more. I think the one in Denmark is actually part park. . . . I started checking a few of those as I went through Europe. I know it's weird. I wasn't fascinated with death. It was from an architectural point of view. Funereal works are psychologically and emotionally based, and I was very interested in the psychological effects architecture has on people.

Lin traveled to other countries, as well. She visited the Acropolis in Athens, where she saw the Parthenon, the ancient temple dedicated to Athena. She also studied the spare, modern buildings by Ludwig Mies Van Der Rohe and Walter Gropius, German architects who fled to the United States in the 1930s. Finally, she saw World War I memorials in France. "For the first time, they focused on human lives lost, focused on the loss of individual life," Lin explained. "Before the twentieth century, your average foot soldier didn't count."

person—the more she looked like the very enemy they had been fighting in the first place.

The truth was, this memorial was unlike any war memorial ever built. As the judges had predicted when they selected the winner, the design created controversy. The judges themselves, who were sophisticated, academically trained experts, saw great merit in Lin's effort. Some of the vets, however—like the man testifying before the Fine Arts Commission—complained that the design focused on death and defeat, and demeaned their sacrifice.

Lin was a force to be reckoned with, though. She was only 5 feet, 3 inches tall and weighed less than 100 pounds (45.4 kilograms), but she stood up to her critics and defended her concept. She spoke up at the hearings; she explained her point of view in the newspapers and on TV.

The members of the Vietnam Veterans Memorial Fund, as well as the expert judges, stood by their winner. They pointed out that there was no political message intended in the memorial. They only wanted to honor all Vietnam vets—people who they felt had been largely ignored since the war ended. The vets had not chosen the design. An impartial jury of experts selected the winner. Further, as Jan Scruggs pointed out, "Some of the finest architects in the country, some of the highest-priced architectural firms in the country did enter this competition."

Indeed, Lin's own college professor had entered the contest. The entries were blind. The names of the people who submitted the designs were hidden. The works were judged strictly on their own merits.

In the end, most veteran organizations, including the American Legion and the Veterans of Foreign Wars, continued to support the VVMF and Lin's design. The celebrities and politicians who had supported the effort—including former First Lady Rosalynn Carter and then-current First Lady Nancy Reagan—stood by their initial beliefs.

Contributions came in from all corners of the land, from veterans themselves, from the mothers and fathers of slain soldiers, from charitable organizations, and from private corporations. The Veterans of Foreign Wars presented a check for $180,000. Former Secretary of State Henry Kissinger, the architect of much of American policy during the Vietnam War, made out a personal check for $500. By the time the fundraising drive was over, about 275,000 people had responded with contributions large and small. The entire $7 million necessary to build the monument was raised, and the Vietnam Veterans Memorial never cost the government a dime.

Jan Scruggs gave credit to Lin, as quoted in Bob Italia's book *Maya Lin*:

> She really stood by her guns to make sure that this memorial design was not tampered with. And it was very important that she did that, because throughout the entire controversy that surrounded the memorial, she really believed in this design. She really knew it was going to work. . . . The strength of her own convictions carried us through quite a few conflicts.

The memorial still needed the approval of Secretary of the Interior James Watt, however. He insisted the VVMF consider the objections from the critics. He insisted they all reach a compromise.

Some critics wanted the names of those killed to be presented in alphabetical order, so they would be easy to locate. But Lin argued that the power of the memorial depended on the historical context. There would be a directory, she explained. When people had to locate the name in the directory and then find the name on the wall, it would almost seem like they were finding bodies on a battlefield.

Critics took the trouble to examine the lists of soldiers who had been killed, then they changed their point of view. There were more than 600 Smiths on the lists, and 16 people were named James Jones. An alphabetical listing would look too much like a telephone book. They admitted that Lin was right.

On the other hand, Lin had originally designed the wall with no inscription, no words except the names of the dead. She felt the names spoke for themselves. The critics felt the wall needed some sort of explanation to make it clear that the memorial was honoring not just the dead, but all those who served. This time Lin compromised, allowing a short prologue and a brief epilogue.

As for the issue of color, that was settled at a meeting when General George Price, one of America's highest-ranking black officers, reminded everyone of the sacrifice that Martin Luther King, Jr., had made in his fight for justice. "Black is not a color of shame," said Price. "Color meant nothing on the battlefields of Korea and Vietnam. We are all equal in combat. Color should mean nothing now." After that, no one objected to the color black.

There was still the need to satisfy those vets who felt Lin's design was too depressing, too . . . underground. Her opponents wanted a memorial that would pay tribute to the heroism of the American soldier. They thought there should at least be an American flag at the site and maybe a statue of a serviceman. For Lin, who wanted to keep politics out of the design, there were still plenty more politics that had to be played out.

4

She Was Right
All Along

Opponents of the Lin design would not quit. They gave ground on the color and the names; they got their way on the inscription. They still worried, however, about the effect of putting the memorial underground, as they saw it. In addition, they asked, wasn't there something that could be done to make the memorial look more patriotic, something that would pay tribute to their sacrifice rather than burying it in shame?

In November 1981, the American Institute of Architects Foundation organized an exhibit of the best designs from the VVMF competition. The second- and third-place entries were featured, along with the 15 honorable mentions and another 43 designs that were judged meritorious.

The press and the art critics all marveled at how Lin's design stood out from the crowd. "Just how wrong are the naysayers and how amazingly right were the jurors can be seen in the exhibition of the winning design and its chief competitors," enthused the *Washington Post*. "Those impressive, long black walls, set into the earth, are perfect. They will invite the viewer to walk down the hill. They will demand a response without dictating what it should be. They will insist simply that he reflect in some way upon the nature of the sacrifices made."

Lin won an award from the American Institute of Architects. Still Ross Perot and friends pressed their opposition. Perot said he had received bundles of letters against the memorial, and only two letters in favor. "Look, let's do one thing right for these men," he said, "these veterans [whom] this country abused when they were in Vietnam and when they came home. Let's have a monument [of] which they can be proud. If they want this design, that's okay, too, but let's find out."

Perot proposed taking a poll of Vietnam vets, asking them if they wanted the Lin design or something else. The VVMF, however, vetoed that suggestion. "How could a fair poll be done about a memorial that was not yet built?" asked Jan Scruggs. "You would wind up with a hundred different groups pushing a hundred different designs—and there would be no memorial."

Scruggs and his colleagues kept pointing out that the memorial was not underground. It would be cut into a slope. The wall would have southern exposure, allowing plenty of sunlight to shine on the wall. Besides, they argued, by keeping the wall low and horizontal, visitors could read the names. If the names went any higher than ten feet (3 m)—on a pillar or obelisk, for example—no one could read the names at the top.

Everyone realized that the stakes were high. "The memorial will occupy a permanence in the national mindset, with an even greater power than history itself," wrote James Webb, a supporter of the memorial, but one who had reservations about Lin's design. "History can be re-evaluated. New facts can be discovered, leading to different interpretations. But a piece of art remains, as a testimony to a particular moment in history, and we are under a solemn obligation to get that moment down as correctly as possible."

Perhaps for that very reason, Maya Lin herself opposed any changes to her design. "It's incredible how possessive I am about the memorial," she confessed. "It's like my art is my babies. . . . Usually creating is such a selfish act. For the first time I created something beyond myself."

And, as young as she was, she also knew that she had it right. She absolutely knew that the veterans who opposed the design misunderstood what she was doing. She meant no disrespect; she had no political agenda. Also, once the memorial was built, she knew these people would feel the power of the wall as much as anyone else.

Lin said later in an interview with Bill Moyers, "If I was a Vietnam veteran and someone said, 'You're getting a ditch, a black ditch,'—if that's what I read, I wouldn't want it either. I could understand people not getting what it would be . . . [but] I was never afraid that it wouldn't work. . . . I am very focused. And some would say extremely stubborn. And you kind of know when you've hit it, you know when it's right."

The VVMF wanted to get the memorial built in time to dedicate it on Veterans Day. Opposition to the design was stalling the whole process, however. Scruggs worried that the controversy would mean that the memorial wouldn't get built on time, or maybe not at all.

A meeting was arranged between the supporters and the opponents of the memorial, set for January 27, 1982. About 100 people showed up. Lin was not invited.

The debate between the two sides went on for hours. All the pros and cons of the design were reviewed and rehashed. Finally a general who supported the memorial stood up. He said the arguments had gone on long enough. It was time for compromise.

He suggested the VVMF add a statue to the design and find a place for an American flag. Could everyone live with that? Suddenly, a compromise seemed possible. Yes, it was time to pull together. The opponents allowed that as long as there was a statue and a flag, they would halt their efforts to block the memorial. The VVMF also agreed. There was a voice vote. The "ayes" had it.

The VVMF would go back and review submissions to the design competition, looking for a suitable statue. Exactly where the flag and the statue would be located . . . that was a decision left for another time.

Jan Scruggs had to break the news to Lin. "Aesthetically, the design does not need a statue," he told her, "but politically it does." She realized that there wasn't much he could have done about it and agreed to go along with the new configuration. The VVMF then took the new proposal through the Washington bureaucracy.

The National Capital Planning Commission approved. The Fine Arts Commission approved. And on March 15, 1982, Secretary of the Interior James Watt finally signed off on the building permit. Construction could begin.

On March 26, 1982, about 500 feet (150 m) of red ribbon were laid out across the grounds of Constitution Gardens on the Washington Mall, along the lines that Lin had marked off the previous fall. One arm of the ribbon pointed toward the Washington Monument, the other toward the Lincoln Memorial. More than 100 shovels—one each for representatives of the 50 states and all the major veterans organizations—dotted the length of the ribbon. It was the ground-breaking ceremony for the Vietnam Veterans Memorial.

A group of officials huddled around the podium, while several thousand spectators attended the ceremony. Bulldozers stood by to begin their assault on the earth. Pile drivers were at the ready behind them, to sink 140 concrete pilings into bedrock to support the wall.

Charles Hagel, deputy administrator of the Veterans Administration—and now a U.S. senator from Nebraska—recalled his tour of duty in Vietnam and implored everyone to also remember the 2,500 soldiers that at the time were still missing in

Frederic K. Hart described the motivation for his statue *Three Fighting Men*:
"I see the wall as a kind of ocean, a sea of sacrifice that is overwhelming and
nearly incomprehensible in its sweep of names...I place these figures upon
the shore of that sea, gazing upon it, standing vigil before it, reflecting the
human face of it, the human heart."

action (MIA) in Southeast Asia. "We must know, and understand, that there is no glory in war, only suffering," he told the crowd. "That's why we recognize those who have gone before us and that's why we continually try and understand and learn from wars."

Meantime, Lin and the architectural firm were hard at work bringing the design to life. The walls of the memorial had to be lengthened to allow for all the names, in part because it was decided the names of the MIAs would be included with those who were killed. They, too, would be presented in chronological order, placed in the wall at the time they went missing.

Lin devised a system for marking each name with one of two symbols. The confirmed dead would be marked with a diamond; the missing with a cross. Then, if a missing person was confirmed dead, the cross would be filled in to complete the diamond. If a missing person was ever found alive, the cross would be inscribed with a circle.

The builders of the memorial worked with the U.S. Department of Defense to create the official list of names and their dates of death. The VVMF checked and cross-checked the casualty lists to make sure all the eligible names were included—and that the names were spelled correctly.

The black granite for the wall had to come from outside the United States, because all the granite quarried there has prominent gray veins. Both Canada and Sweden had quarries of beautiful black granite that Lin thought would be perfect. The veterans vetoed the idea of procuring granite from either Canada or Sweden, however, because a number of draft evaders had fled there during the Vietnam era.

A quarry near Bangalore, India, finally produced the granite for the wall. About 3,000 cubic feet (84.9 cubic meters) of stone, weighing 300 tons (272.1 metric tons), were shipped to the United States and trucked to a stone fabricator in Vermont. Using diamond-tipped saws, stonecutters fashioned the granite blocks into 150 panels—each 40 inches (102 cm) wide and only 3 inches (7.6 cm) thick.

Lin did not want a thick wall, only a thin veneer. "I always saw the wall as a pure surface," she wrote, "an interface between light and dark, where I cut the earth and polished its open edge. The wall dematerializes as a form and allows the names to become the object, a pure and reflective surface that would allow visitors the chance to see themselves with the names."

The height of the panels would vary. The tallest, destined for the center of the memorial, rose up to 10 feet, 8 inches (3.2 m). The smallest, the ones on the ends, were cut down to a less than a foot. Skilled laborers polished each of the slices, using a series of bricks that worked like sandpaper. They then buffed the surface of each panel to a glossy finish.

When all was ready, workers wrapped up the shiny panels in protective material and delivered them to be engraved at a glassworks factory in Memphis, Tennessee. Stonecutters cleaned each panel and coated it with chemicals. Then, using stencils of the names generated by the defense department, the workers covered the panel with the photographic negatives consisting of a list of the names in chronological order, exactly as they would appear on the wall. Each panel was left in the light and washed again, leaving the names on the shiny black surface. The stonecutters then sandblasted the names into the panel by hand.

Meanwhile, back in Washington, the veterans from the VVMF turned their attention to the compromise they had made. They had to come up with a statue of a soldier to go with Maya Lin's wall. They asked Frederick Hart, the Washington sculptor who had placed third in the competition, to come up with a proposal. Hart was happy to oblige, and he produced a realistic model of three battle-weary soldiers—one black, one white, and one Hispanic—who were presumably returning from patrol. The three men were young, but they looked exhausted as they gazed off into the distance.

A U.S. Navy officer and the Washington Monument are reflected in the black granite surface of the Vietnam Veterans Memorial.

Many veterans thought Hart's sculpture successfully captured a feel for their time in Vietnam. More important, the
VVMF wanted to get the memorial built, and built on time.
They had agreed to a compromise, and the Hart statue seemed
fine to them. They went ahead and commissioned the work, a

Being Asian American — FINDING HER WAY

Maya Lin called her book *Boundaries*, because she feels she lives
and works between two worlds: between East and West, between
science and intuition, between art and architecture, between the
established order of things and being an outsider.

Lin has always felt like an outsider, even as a child. She had
few friends in Athens, Ohio, and she didn't fit into the social scene
at school. As she told PBS interviewer Bill Moyers: "I was so mis-
erable by the time I got to high school, and so I had pretty much re-
treated into my own world. . . . I was really out of place. And I didn't
understand why I was out of place. I mean, it seems so obvious.
But if you're going through it you don't have a clue. If I look back I
was probably an incredible misfit. I had friends but it wasn't like I
belonged. I didn't want to date. I just wanted to study."

As Lin grew older, she became more aware of her Chinese
heritage and how it separated her from the American mainstream.
As she reflected for an interview with National Public Radio:

> I think that I, growing up, picked up my father and mother's
> feelings of being immigrants, that there has been throughout
> my life a sense that, you know, "Where am I from?" People,
> without realizing what they are doing, will come up and say to
> me, "Where are you from?" I say, "Ohio." They say, "Where are
> you really from?" which leads you to think that as they look at
> you, no matter how many generations of my family are born
> here, I'm not allowed to be truly from here. What does it do to
> someone's aesthetic?

bronze statue, slightly larger than life-size, to be placed some-where around the wall.

Lin, however, still bristled at the idea of adding another element to her design. She felt that she had won the competition, fair and square, and she thought she was being double-crossed

She recalled the surprise she felt when confronted with the fact of her heritage. In 2000, she told an interviewer:

My parents had emigrated from China. I was not brought up bilingual. I was brought up "white." I think my parents made a choice. It was at a time [that] they wanted us to fit in. So we fit in. Almost to the point where I was in total denial. "Nope, I'm just like everybody else, I'm from Athens, Ohio." When I was 21 or 22, a reporter was going: "Oh, but the Memorial is so Asian." And I said, "Well, you're a Taoist; you're reading your Taoist thoughts into it." It took me another ten years to realize how much my work is as much about Asian or Eastern thought processes. I'm not learned [in Asian philosophy]. But I almost had a knee-jerk reaction against a lot of Western European architectural thought.

And so Lin is a hybrid, the product of an American childhood, but an Asian heritage. "My parents very much brought us up to decide what we wanted to do, and when we wanted to study," she recalled of her childhood. "There was very little discipline, and yet I don't think we ever did anything that was irresponsible. Maybe that is an Eastern philosophy—that you don't force an opinion on a child. You allow them to draw their own conclusions."

"My pieces are always about contradiction," she summed up. "I'm torn between Eastern and Western influences, so there's the yin and the yang, the hard and the soft."

by Washington politicians. She accused Hart of trying to undermine her artistic work, of "drawing moustaches on other people's portraits."

Even more disturbing to Lin was the proposed placement of the sculpture, as well as the flag. The most vocal opponents of her design wanted them positioned in the center, where the two walls would meet at the V. Lin was horrified at this idea. The heads of the statue would stick up above the memorial, disturbing the sight lines of the wall. She charged, too, that the placement of the flag at the top of the V would look ridiculous. They would make the memorial look like the putting green on a golf course.

The issue came to a head, once again, at the Fine Arts Commission. Lin and the art experts pleaded with the commission to leave the wall alone. This time, however, the VVMF joined forces with opponents of the design, agreeing that the statue would be a suitable addition to the memorial.

The Fine Arts Commission made a field trip to Constitution Gardens and viewed the Vietnam Veterans Memorial, now under construction. They brought with them a model of the Frederick Hart statue, which they moved back and forth along the wall like a homeowner trying to decide where to put a sofa in the living room.

Members of the commission finally voted in favor of the statue. The statue would be built. After further study, though, they agreed to place the statue not in front of the wall, but off to the side, creating a kind of entrance to the gardens.

Lin was not happy, but she was mollified. "In a funny sense the compromise brings the memorial closer to the truth," Lin later wrote. "What is also memorialized is that people still cannot resolve that war, nor can they separate the issues, the politics, from it."

The VVMF planned a five-day-long National Salute to Vietnam Veterans for November 1982—a hero's welcome to the veterans who didn't get one when they first came home.

People traveled to Washington, D.C., from all over the country. They came by bus, by car, and by airplane. One vet walked 3,000 miles (4,800 kilometers), dressed in combat fatigues and carrying a full military pack.

About 250 volunteers gathered at the National Cathedral to read aloud the names of those killed in Vietnam. It would take more than 50 hours to get through all the names. President Ronald Reagan stopped by for a short while and listened to the reading.

The Salute included ceremonies at Arlington Cemetery, reunions for army units, and receptions for former prisoners of war. In all, more than 150,000 people journeyed to Washington that week—and while they were there, they discovered the wall.

Parents arrived to search for the names of their sons. Children saw the names of their fathers. Veterans themselves gathered to find the names of friends. They came in the daylight and saw their own faces reflected back by the shiny black granite. They came at night and read the names by flashlight, by candlelight, and by the light of a struck match.

All of them felt compelled to touch the wall. They ran their fingers across the cold stone, feeling the edges of these engraved names that were less than an inch tall. Some of those fingers lingered over the letters, as if touching the name could bring that person back to life. Others would touch the wall and pull away, as if the stone was hot.

The people stared. They made chalk rubbings of the surface. They held small flags. They left flowers. They took pictures. Many family members—standing alone, or holding on to one another in small groups—broke down and cried as they remembered their loved ones, the sons, brothers, and fathers who were gone. Many of the vets themselves, recalling their comrades, reliving those months in the jungles of Southeast Asia, held on to one another and wept openly, unashamed of the emotions that overwhelmed them.

On Saturday, November 13, thousands of veterans marched in a parade, past the White House, down Constitution Avenue to the dedication ceremonies of the Vietnam Veterans Memorial. There were speeches from politicians, commanders, and generals. The crowd sang "God Bless America."

Jan Scruggs stood up. "After graduating from high school, I was among the thousands who volunteered for Vietnam," he told the crowd. "Half the men I served with were killed or wounded. When I returned I found that being known as a Vietnam veteran was a dubious distinction."

He went on, "We've waited a long time for this kind of welcome and this kind of memorial. Let it recognize the Vietnam veterans' service. Let it begin the healing process and let it stand as a symbol of national unity."

The Vietnam Veterans Memorial was dedicated, but its impact was just beginning. Two years later, during another Veterans Day ceremony, the Frederick Hart statue was officially added to the memorial, a respectful distance down the Mall.

Since then, the memorial has been the most visited site in the nation's capital, drawing up to 15,000 visitors a day. Every year, more than a million people find their way to Constitution Gardens. They cast a glance at the statue of the three soldiers, then they walk solemnly to the wall that emerges from the ground. They make their way slowly along the black edge of the wall, until it rises above them, blocking out the city. They touch the stone; they feel the names; they remember the men and the war and the unsettled times.

They also leave behind mementos of their loved ones. They make offerings of flowers and notes at the base of the memorial. They carefully place a hat or a boot or an item of clothing on the ground; sometimes they leave a ribbon or a medal or a personal item, offered up to the memory of the Vietnam War and the men who died there.

"The piece was built as a very psychological memorial," says Lin. "It's not meant to be cheerful or happy, but to bring out in

The dedication ceremony for the Vietnam Veterans Memorial in Washington, D.C., on November 13, 1982, was attended by more than 150,000 people.

people the realization of loss and a cathartic healing process. A lot of people were really afraid of that emotion; it was something we had glossed over."

Lin's vision, as she first imagined it back in 1980 when she made her visit to the Mall on that crisp November day, continues to work its magic. She was right all along.

A Girl From Ohio

Maya Lin was one of very few Asian Americans growing up in Athens, Ohio, in the 1960s. But she says she was almost completely unaware of her Chinese heritage. She assumed she was just like everyone else, living in a small, white, clapboard house with lots of windows that offered views of the hills and woods on the outskirts of a typical American town.

Lin's parents were from China, making Maya the first generation in her family to be born in the United States. Her father, Henry Huan Lin, came to America from a prominent family in Beijing. Henry Lin's father—Maya's grandfather—was named Lin Chang-min. He was a lawyer who supported progressive causes, and in the early 1900s he helped write one of the first constitutions in modern Chinese history.

China was embroiled in revolutionary activities during those years, fighting to free itself from foreign influence and a corrupt old empire. Lin Chang-min was involved with the Nationalist Party, which overthrew the ancient Chinese dynasty, established an independent government, and later fought against the Japanese in World War II. After the war, however, the Nationalists lost out to the Communists, who fought their way to power in the 1940s and, in a much-altered form, continue to rule China today.

Maya Lin's grandfather served as a cabinet member in the independent Chinese government. In 1921, he was sent to London to represent China at the League of Nations, a precursor to the United Nations. In England, he traveled in circles that included famous politicians and literary lights of the time, including H.G. Wells, Thomas Hardy, Bertrand Russell, and an influential Chinese poet by the name of Hsu Chih-mo.

Lin Chang-min returned to China, where he and his family continued an active involvement in national affairs. Maya Lin's father, Henry Huan Lin, grew up to become an academic administrator in Beijing, as well an accomplished artist working in pottery and ceramics.

When it became evident that the Communists would take over the government, young Henry Lin, like many of those associated with the Nationalists, decided to flee the country. With the aid of some friends, he made his way to America.

Lin landed at the University of Washington, in Seattle, and later was able to find a position on the faculty of Ohio University, in Athens. He became a professor of art, and later, by the time Maya Lin was a little girl, he had moved up to become dean of the fine arts program at the university.

Lin's mother, Julia Chang, also hailed from a prominent family in China. She was the daughter of an influential physician in Shanghai. In 1948, as the Communists battled their way to power, attacking Shanghai and raining bombs down on the city, young Julia was spirited out of the country, reportedly fleeing with only a single $100 bill pinned into the lining of her coat.

Friends of the family helped Julia get to America. People sympathetic to the Nationalist cause came to her aid and encouraged her to head to Northampton, Massachusetts, where she was granted a scholarship to Smith College.

Julia Chang graduated from Smith in 1951. She soon moved to Seattle and began postgraduate work at the University of Washington. That's where she met Henry Lin. They married, and when Henry Lin was offered a job in Ohio, the young couple settled in Athens.

Julia Chang Lin joined her new husband on the faculty of the university, teaching English and Oriental literature. She became a respected professor in her own right and went on to publish several academic books on modern Chinese poetry. She also wrote and published a number of her own poems.

In 1956, the couple had their first child, a son they named Tan. Their daughter came along three years later; she was born on October 5, 1959. They named her Maya Ying Lin.

The word *ying* is Chinese for jade, a precious stone; *Lin* means "forest". Maya is not a Chinese name. It's the name of Buddha's mother. "It means illusion," Julia Lin explained to a *Washington Post* reporter after her daughter became famous. "Life is an illusion, everything is emptiness. I chose that name for her because it's beautiful and I'm a little bit of a Buddhist. Also a friend of mine at Smith had that name, a beautiful Indian girl."

Although the Lin family assimilated into American culture, the parents clearly passed on to Maya an Eastern view of the world—whether Maya knew it or not. It was a close-knit family, and the two children showed interest in their parents' activities. Both her parents were academics, and they were also artists. Henry Lin, the father, was an accomplished potter, ceramicist, and furniture maker. Maya grew up eating from the stoneware plates and bowls that her father made by hand. She sat at tables fashioned by her father in his workshop.

Maya's mother was a poet, and although Maya took after her father, her brother followed in his mother's literary footsteps. Older brother Tan wrote poetry as a child and attended

Between the Generations
MAYA LIN'S FAMOUS AUNT

When Maya Lin's grandfather, Lin Chang-min, traveled to London in 1921, he brought with him his daughter, Lin Hui-yin. The young woman, 17 years old at the time, was Henry Lin's older half-sister . . . Maya Lin's aunt.

While in London, grandfather Lin Chang-min met a young Chinese writer, Hsu Chih-mo, the son of a wealthy Chinese merchant, and the two men became fast friends. Hsu had spent two years in the United States pursuing degrees in politics and economics, but in 1920 he had given that up to follow a more idealistic path. He moved first to literary London, and then he enrolled in Cambridge University, where he studied English literature and read Romantic poets such as Percy Bysshe Shelley, John Keats, and Lord Byron.

Hsu Chih-mo was married, and with his wife he moved into a house outside Cambridge. The poet was taken with Lin Chang-min's daughter, however. According to historian Jonathan Spence, Hsu "in his restless and excitable state, found in the young Miss Lin a soul mate who also happened to be a beautiful and widely traveled young woman."

In short, Hsu fell madly in love with the teenager, and soon the two of them were meeting for tea in the afternoons. After Hsu moved to Cambridge, they exchanged letters every day. Hsu used a local grocery store as his mailing address, to keep the affair hidden from his wife. Every day he would bicycle to the store to send off his love letter and retrieve a much-anticipated note from young Lin Hui-yin.

It wasn't long before Hsu's wife realized what was going on. She left her husband, taking their son, and the next year they began divorce proceedings. Lin Hui-yin's father also caught on to the situation, and he soon spirited his beautiful daughter back to China. After returning home, Lin Chang-min informally arranged for a marriage between his daughter and the son of an old friend, a man named Liang Si-cheng.

About a year later, Hsu Chih-mo returned to China and tried to rekindle the flame with Maya Lin's aunt. He had the idea that the two of them would pick up where they'd left off, that they would get married and he would bring her back to England. Lin Hui-yin married Liang Si-cheng, however.

Hsu Chih-mo went on to become a famous writer, attacking traditional Chinese customs and embracing the more free-wheeling Western ways. Meanwhile, Lin Hui-yin and her husband also traveled to the United States, where they studied architecture at the University of Pennsylvania. Lin Hui-yin also spent a semester at Yale, at the school of drama, studying stage design.

Lin Hui-yin and her husband returned to China and established themselves as noted architects and architectural historians. They helped build Tiananmen Square, in the capital of Beijing, and spent much of their lives preserving and documenting historically significant Chinese buildings.

Wilma Fairbank, the wife of a noted Chinese scholar at Harvard University, characterized Lin Hui-yin as "one of those people that you meet at times in artists' groups who could go in any direction: a gifted designer, artist, and poet. At the same time she wrote prose, [she] was a very able architect and a very enchanting person, very pretty and lively and always the center of any group."

Henry Lin, younger brother of Lin Hui-yin, always said that his daughter Maya reminded him of his half sister. "Maya is very emotional, very sensitive. She was always interested in the arts but at the same time all the female Lins are very strong, very independent: all very talented and very determined."

Columbia University in New York. Now, as an adult, Tan Lin has become a published poet and teaches poetry and creative writing at the university level.

While Maya was growing up, the Lin household was full of books and magazines and arts and crafts. Maya was encouraged to develop her mind, sharpen her skills—and follow her passions and search for the true path of her life. "My parents never directly told us what to do but rather let my brother and me make our own choices," said Lin. She was encouraged to learn and experiment and find "the passages to an awareness, to what my mother would describe in Taoism as 'the Way.'"

Maya was shy and withdrawn in school. But she didn't feel different because she was Asian in a mostly white school. She felt different because she was not interested in boys. She felt different because, unlike the popular girls, she was not fascinated by fashion. She didn't date, didn't wear makeup. And as a mark of her individuality, Maya let her hair grow long, until it was down to her waist.

Maya did dress in jeans and T-shirts and sneakers, like a lot of the other kids. She also worked at McDonald's for a while, because that was the only place around Athens where a kid could get a job, and she wanted to make some money.

Instead of spending a lot of time hanging out at friends' houses, though, Maya would entertain herself at home. She would beg her father to let her come to his studio, where she would watch him at the pottery wheel. She also liked to get her hands on the clay and throw a bowl or fire a pot, and she was an apt pupil at her father's knee.

At home, Maya played games with her brother. She especially enjoyed chess. She also spent a lot of time by herself, doing her homework and making things with her hands. As a young girl, she would construct paper houses and villages in her room. As she got older, she worked on sculpture and ceramics and tried her hand at silversmithing.

Maya preferred reading to watching television. She was drawn to fantasy fiction by C.S. Lewis and J.R.R. Tolkien, as well as stories from Greek mythology. As she got older, she turned to the existentialists, such as French writers Albert Camus and Jean Paul Sartre. She never read much about current events, though, and she was not particularly interested in what was going on in China or the Far East.

Maya also spent hours exploring the family's backyard. She liked nature and would sit still and watch the rabbits and squirrels, the chipmunks and raccoons. She roamed the woods behind her house, which were laced with small streams, and discovered ancient Indian burial mounds. There were three distinct hills rising up in back of her yard. "I called the middle one the 'lizard's back' because it started up from the creek bed, like a tail. It grew into a long winding ridge, and ended in what to us looked like the head of a lizard."

Secluded at home, wrapped up in family activities, Maya led a sheltered life, barely aware of the political turmoil going on around her in the 1960s. She hated war and violence; she didn't even like violent movies. Art and literature were a part of her daily life, but politics was not.

When she was a little girl, the civil rights struggle was going on in the South, with protests and demonstrations and marches. She was eight years old when civil rights activist Reverend Martin Luther King, Jr., was shot and killed. She did not pay much attention to the news, though—she was caught up in her own world.

During Maya's elementary- and middle-school years, there were demonstrations against the Vietnam War at Ohio University and elsewhere. The historic Kent State massacre, when the Ohio National Guard killed four students at an antiwar protest, took place when Maya was 10 years old, fewer than 200 miles (322 kilometers) from her home. Lin's parents kept her inside when the rare demonstration flooded into the streets in Athens. She didn't understand the significance of the protests. She never

Ohio National Guardsmen patrol the empty Kent State University campus following student protests against the Vietnam War. On that day—May 6, 1970—four people were killed and ten were injured.

read about the war, and later she never watched movies about the Vietnam War.

Maya always knew that she would grow up to be a professional woman, like her mother. She never felt she was treated differently in her family because she was a girl. Her mother, reflected Maya, "worked on her books and on her teaching career and took care of us. So whether I would work was never an issue; only what my work would be."

Meanwhile, in school Maya was an excellent student. When she was young, she went to an experimental elementary school at the university. Then she attended public high school in Athens, but she continued her connection to Ohio University, taking college-level courses in computers and science. Math was her favorite subject, and she loved solving trigonometry problems. "I find it very fun to be thinking all the time, figuring things out," she later revealed. "I guess you could say I was somewhat of a nerd."

She was also, by her own admission, a teacher's pet. There was one chemistry teacher in particular who took her under her wing. They would stay after school and do extra chemistry experiments. On at least one occasion they almost got into trouble. They stuffed a pot with flash powder and set it off. The explosion brought the head science teacher running into the room, asking what on earth was going on. Both Maya and the teacher just looked at him and shrugged their shoulders. Everything was fine, they insisted; nothing was wrong. Meanwhile, Maya couldn't hear a thing. The blast had temporarily blown out her hearing.

Lin graduated as the covaledictorian of her class, sharing top honors with one of her classmates. She was accepted at Yale University, in New Haven, Connecticut, one of the most prestigious academic institutions in the country.

When Lin got to Yale for her freshman year, in the fall of 1977, she quickly realized that this was the first place other than home that she felt really comfortable and happy. The professors and her classmates appreciated her creativity and shared her love of learning. She made friends more easily than she had at school in Ohio. She still liked to read, and she would also go for long walks in and around the university, exploring the city of New Haven like she had explored the woods behind her house in Athens. Sometimes she took photographs, but more often she was just interested in getting away from campus and giving herself time to think.

On her walks around New Haven, she discovered the Grove Street Cemetery, an oasis of grass and trees in the middle of the city. "The Grove Street Cemetery is beautiful," she later said. "There's something peaceful about it. You feel removed. You're in the world of the dead."[6] Like many college students, Lin contemplated the meaning of death, but it was always abstract to her—no one close to her had ever died.

"Friends and architects who knew her at Yale," according to Phil McCombs in the *Washington Post*, "describe Lin as powerfully artistic, emotional, fiercely independent, driven: intuitive and personal in her approach to art."

Lin didn't know what her career path would be, however. During her first two years at Yale, she studied a wide range of liberal arts. She liked literature and philosophy, but was especially drawn to the sciences. She thought she might want to be a veterinarian or a zoologist. Then she found out that she'd have to not only autopsy dead animals but also experiment on live ones. She quickly gave up that idea.

She also took several photography courses. "It's something I really enjoy," she said, "along with doing my own cooking and making my own clothes, which, incidentally, I find I like better than anything I can buy."

Lin actually did not even take an architecture course during her first two years in college. She knew she liked art, though, and she liked math. Then one day she was sitting in the college library. "I was just staring up at the ceiling, at all the lines and painting on it and the like, and, suddenly, I decided I was going to be an architect. Just like that."

Once she did enter the architecture program, she says, "I just focused, and I did nothing but." She realized that designing things was in her blood, in her genes, and she spent all her time thinking about art and architecture. And the rest is history.

6

Striking Out
on Her Own

Maya Lin spent about a year in Washington, D.C., through the summer and fall of 1981 and the spring of 1982, watching over the progress of the Vietnam Veterans Memorial. It didn't take her long, however, to grow disillusioned with the politics swirling around her wall and the special interests tugging and pulling at her design. Even before the memorial was finished, Maya decided to return to school to get her master's degree in architecture.

In the summer of 1982, she left Washington to teach at a school in New Hampshire. In the fall, she enrolled at Harvard University, and for several months she went to classes in Boston while commuting down to Washington on weekends to complete her work on the memorial.

The frenetic schedule of this life, however, soon tested her patience and her persistence. She also longed to go back to Yale University, she dropped out of the program at Harvard, applied to the architectural school at Yale, and in the meantime landed a temporary job at an architectural firm in Boston to get some practical experience.

Lin was accepted at Yale, and in the fall of 1983 she went back to New Haven. She spent the next three years working on her master's degree. "I needed a place to start over," she explained. "Yale was like going home."

The professors encouraged her to specialize in one category—either art or architecture— but she resisted. "I would look at my professors, smile, and go about my business. . . . I consider myself both an artist and an architect. I don't combine them, but each informs the other. Architecture, you can say, is like writing a book. Everything in a building matters, from the doorknobs to the paint details. And sculpture is like writing a poem. You're not saying as much. It's an idea stripped bare."

There was one professor, a noted architect named Frank Gehry, who told her to ignore the pressure to specialize and just make the things she wanted to make. It was "the best advice . . . I've ever been given from the architectural world."

Lin did take the required architecture courses. She also spent time in the sculpture department, however. And while at Yale, she met a fellow architectural student, Peter Boynton. "When we started going out," she said, "we decided to do an art and architecture collaboration. We argued for two weeks and almost didn't build it, because we were so different."

The two of them were planning to build a tree house together in Vermont. The structure was supposed to wind along the ground in the woods, and then rise up some 40 feet (12 m) into the trees, and symbolize how two artists collaborate. "But we started having these art arguments," Lin related. "Peter was very expressionistic. We finally just looked at each other glaringly one day, and Peter said, 'Okay, what's more beautiful, the human figure or a pencil?'

"And I looked at him and said, 'A pencil!'

"He said, 'That's it! We're not doing this and I'm not going out with you!'

"And I said, 'Wait a second,' and tried to explain why I thought abstractions can be more beautiful than reality."

One of the unique works Lin did while at Yale was a landscape piece she created in the bend of a small river outside of New Haven. (The art has since disappeared.) She planted a series of tall, thin aluminum rods, painted blue and black, into the mud along the bank of the river, amid a stand of naturally occurring reeds. The rods blended into the reeds. Unless you looked carefully, you wouldn't even notice them. "It was the insertion of a barely perceptible ordering of the natural environment," she later explained.

After she completed the work, which she called "Aligned Reeds," Lin traveled to the site one day. She saw some fishermen standing around scratching their heads, asking, "What is it? Is it alive?" Lin did not let on that she had anything to do with the situation. "They turned to me and said, 'Do you know what it is?' And I said, 'No I don't,' then walked away."

She explained her philosophy: "It's a belief I have: the insertion or intrusion of a quiet order. If you are paying attention, you may notice it; if not, you won't. It's indicative of how I like to work with a site: creating a work that quietly merges with its site so that there remains an ambiguity if it is man-made or a naturally occurring phenomenon."

Lin graduated from Yale School of Architecture in 1986. She received an honorary doctorate from Yale the following year, in recognition of her contribution to the world of art, even at such a young age. She was 27 years old at the time but already one of the university's most famous alumni. She also won a Presidential Design Award, in 1988, and went on to receive numerous other awards and honors.

After graduating from Yale, Lin moved to New York City and tried to live a quiet, creative life with Peter Boynton, who,

A TRIP TO ASIA

In 1985, between semesters at graduate school, Maya visited Asia with her mother and her brother Tan. Henry and Julia Lin had finally decided that the children should know where their parents grew up and what their heritage was all about. Henry was suffering ill health, however, so he stayed home. (Henry Lin died in 1989.)

The three pilgrims visited Julia's relatives. Then they made their way to Fukien Province and the home of Maya's grandfather, where Henry Lin had lived as a boy before moving to Beijing. Maya was surprised that the house was a Japanese-style home. She exclaimed, "I was astonished. It was a house overlooking the river with two or three courtyards. The rooms were not compartmentalized; spaces flowed through sliding screens, treating the architecture as a passageway. It was just magical. I was blown away. I had an affinity to this place. The simplicity and clarity of it, the path."

Maya reported that one reason her mother wanted to go to China in the summer was to get away from the hot, muggy summer of southeastern Ohio, where it's "100 percent humidity and 100 degrees. It is a swamp," according to Maya, "So we are in China, in the summer, in Fukien, and it is identical. And we all started laughing because it's like, 'Of course, Dad found the one place that reminded him of home.'"

While in Asia, Lin did a brief internship with a Japanese architect in Tokyo. She also visited Hong Kong, where she saw two new skyscrapers being built on the waterfront.

Later, back home in America, Lin published a critique of the modern skyscraper and pointed to these two new buildings as refreshing developments in the current cityscape. "The emergence of these two spectacular new buildings amid the dreary, mirrored glass boxes and computer punch card blocks . . . promises a sci-fi look that will startle the unsuspecting visitor to Hong Kong," she wrote. "Both will stand in the front of the harbor, straight ahead as one approaches the island from the mainland, welcoming not just to the island but to the twenty-first century."

as it turned out, had continued to go out with her. They lived in a loft on the Bowery in downtown Manhattan. Their building was populated with other artists, and Maya and Peter together adopted a couple of cats.

One end of the loft served as Lin's office and studio; it was dotted with machines and sprinkled with sketches, plans, and blueprints. The other end provided a sparsely furnished living area. There was also an adjacent workshop, where both Boynton and Lin experimented with various materials and compositions.

Occasionally, Lin would grant an interview or agree to give a talk. For the most part, though, she now lived and worked out of the public eye. She dressed inconspicuously in worn jeans and old sneakers. She cut her signature long hair to above her shoulders. "You really can't function as a celebrity," she said. "Entertainers are celebrities. I'm an architect. I'm an artist. I make things. I just love the fact that I can make a work and put it out there and walk away from it and then look at it like everyone else."

And so Lin set to work. She was paying her dues, working toward an internship at an architectural firm in New York. She spent time renovating a house in Connecticut. She also labored over her sculptures, including a series of small compositions made of glass, wood, wax, and lead. One piece, made to hang from a wall, consisted of a slab of beeswax, crisscrossed with veins of lead. "It's 5 feet 3 inches tall and 95 pounds," she offered, "the same height and weight as me."

One day in the spring of 1988, Lin was home sick with the flu when the phone rang. It was a representative of the Southern Poverty Law Center (SPLC) in Montgomery, Alabama. Founded in 1971, the SPLC is an organization that advances the rights of minorities. The board of directors, the representative explained, had decided they wanted to place a memorial to the civil rights struggle at the entrance to their headquarters. They'd immediately thought of Maya Lin. They'd been calling every Lin in New York, until they finally got her on the phone.

"At first I was hesitant to respond," Lin later wrote, "since I was acutely aware of the amount of attention I had received from the Vietnam Veterans Memorial and I did not want to be typecast as a monument builder." When she learned, though, that there was no national memorial to the civil rights movement, her interest was piqued. She agreed to do some research and meet with the people from the center to find out what they had in mind for the project.

The SPLC envisioned a stone plaque mounted at the entrance to their building in Montgomery. It would list the names of 40 or so prominent people who had been killed in the civil rights struggle. Lin realized, however, that just putting the names there would not have much impact. She described her feelings:

> In asking myself the question of what a memorial to civil rights should be, I realized . . . I needed to make people aware of the history of that era. At the same time, I wanted to respond to the future and to the continuing struggle toward racial equality. I could not envision a closed time line, since I couldn't see or feel comfortable saying that the civil rights movement had a set beginning or end.

Lin made a trip to Montgomery to see the site and talk with the directors. The entrance to the building consisted of two flights of stairs curving up to a small landing, and then another flight of stairs leading to the front door. That was a problem, she realized, but when she told the directors she would have to completely rework the front of the building, they signaled that they were willing to work with her.

On her trip to Montgomery, Maya Lin read Martin Luther King, Jr.'s, famous "I Have a Dream" speech from the 1963 march for civil rights in Washington. She read: "With this faith we will be able to hew out of the mountain of despair a stone of hope." That gave her the idea that, like the Vietnam Veterans Memorial, this memorial should be made out of stone, her favorite dark granite. Then she got to the words: "We are not satisfied, we will not be satisfied until justice rolls down like waters and righteousness like a mighty stream."

She knew immediately that the monument would have to incorporate water into its design, and that King's words, adapted from the Bible, would have to be featured on the memorial.

Lin sketched out a design on a napkin and showed it to the members of the center. They agreed with her concept, and so she went back to New York to work on her idea. A few months later, she presented her plans to the public. She explained:

> The memorial divides the entrance to the center into an upper and lower plaza. The upper plaza will contain a quiet pool. A thin sheet of water will flow continuously over the front edge of the pool down the face of the curved wall 9 feet high and 40 feet long and inscribed across the face of the wall will be the words that Dr. Martin Luther King Jr., paraphrased from the Bible. . . . The lower plaza will contain a circular stone table 12 feet in diameter; water emerging from the table center will flow evenly across its surface. Carved beneath the flowing-water concentric-circle time lines will be the story of the civil rights movement and the names of persons killed during the struggle.

The 12-foot (3.6 m) table would sit opposite a single curved stairway on one side of the entrance. The monument would be asymmetrical, but the two main features would balance each other. This was an important element of the design. Lin was trying to convey a basic tenet of her artistic philosophy, an idea that perhaps spilled over to her view of race and national origin—that things, or people, don't have to look exactly the same in order to be equal.

Visitors tour the Civil Rights Memorial outside the Southern Poverty Law
Center in Montgomery, Alabama.

It took Lin a year to finish the project. The Southern Poverty Law Center identified 53 events and 53 names, and she
arranged them chronologically in an open-ended circle that
looks something like a sundial.

The first entry is 17 May 1954, when the U.S. Supreme
Court outlawed school segregation. The last entry is 4 April
1968, the day Martin Luther King was assassinated. A thin
sheet of water falls down the 9-foot (2.7 m) wall, flowing over
the words of Martin Luther King. Another film of water ema-
nates from the table below, spreading over the time line, mak-

ing the top of the table shiny, reflecting the sunlight and the faces reading the history.

About 6,000 people attended the dedication of the memorial, on November 5, 1989, including relatives of those killed in the civil rights struggle and a number of the participants in the events inscribed on the table. "As they gathered around the circle, the circle closed and became more intimate," recalled Lin, "and as the tears that were shed fell onto the table and became part of it, I realized we had all become a part of the shared experience of the memorial."

Even before Lin finished her work on the Civil Rights Memorial, she started getting inquiries about producing other large-scale sculptures. She was anxious to get back to working with landscapes—as she had done with the Vietnam Veterans Memorial, the monument that was cut into the side of a hill— and so she took some opportunities to work on what she termed open, large-scale earth works.

The first was an outdoor peace chapel for Juniata College in Pennsylvania. A man named John Baker was a friend of Lin's parents. He had graduated from Juniata College and was president of Ohio University from 1945 to 1961. After he retired, he went back to Juniata and established a department of peace studies. Now he was donating funds for a peace chapel—a place where people could go to reflect and contemplate, and hold nondenominational church services.

When she visited the site, located in a 400-acre bird sanctuary, Lin saw it was perched on a hill, and there was a wooded ridge several hundred feet away, overlooking the open field. The idea came to her: a sculpture in two parts, with an open public place and a more secluded private spot on the ridge.

As the public place, she designed a circle on the hill, some 40 feet (12 m) in diameter, a grassy area surrounded by a series of small stones. Then, up on the ridge, she placed one solid stone, four feet (1.2 m) in diameter, to provide a more private area for personal reflection. Thus, she merged the public and

The Peace Chapel is an environmental landscape that occupies a 14-acre site within the 170-acre Baker-Henry Nature Preserve near the Juniata College campus in central Pennsylvania.

private, which she felt balanced each other out. Like the Vietnam Veterans Memorial and like "Aligning Reeds," this project seemed to grow out of the landscape and merge with the earth.

Lin's next project, in Charlotte, North Carolina, offered an opportunity to approach the landscape in a more whimsical way. She was asked to design the entrance to a sports complex, the Charlotte Coliseum—perhaps a sculpture to decorate the front entrance of the building. Instead, she decided to incorporate into her design the long driveway leading up to the site.

Lin constructed earthen berms along the driveway. At the top, near the coliseum, she planted two ball-shaped holly trees. Along the berms, she placed other holly trees at strategic locations, looking as though they were balls rolling down the hill, spiraling into an amphitheater at the bottom of the driveway. Lin explained how she felt about the project: "To make something as playful and irreverent as this after the completion of both the Vietnam and Civil Rights memorials was crucial for

Maya Lin and her collaborator, landscape architect Henry Arnold, shaped the 1600-foot median of the approach to the Charlotte (NC) Coliseum with berms and then planted it with 12-foot (3.6-m) Burford holly bushes pruned to look like balls in some outsized mythic game.

me. After creating two memorials, I needed to prove to myself and others that I wasn't going to be stereotyped." She called the work *Topo*. The name suggested topography, of course, but it was also meant to be playful—"like Topo, like a little kids' game," she said.

After North Carolina, Lin was able to come home to Ohio for another sculpture that would blur the line between building and landscape. She was commissioned to produce a piece of art for the rooftop courtyards of the Wexner Center for the Arts at Ohio State University, in Columbus, Ohio. Lin explained this project:

> The museum's director of exhibitions was aware of the smaller studio sculptures that I was always making while working on the larger, more public pieces, small sculptures made from broken glass, beeswax and lead. My interest in working with broken glass in a larger outdoor space had until then been preempted by the inherent danger of leaving accessible broken glass in a public space. Yet on my early visits to the Wexner Center I knew I had the chance to use glass in this sculpture, since the spaces were visible yet inaccessible.

This sculpture was indeed in the "large" category. She ordered more than 40 tons of broken glass, which arrived at the Ohio site in giant dump trucks. Working with the roofing contractor, Lin secured a crane and a large conical bucket. She would fill up a bucket, then pour the glass onto sections of the roof, creating mounds of glass of various shapes and sizes, all merging into one another. The mounds, looking something like sand dunes, covered three separate spaces on three different levels.

She called her work "Groundswell," which as she explained, is an undulation in the ocean, creating not so much a landscape as a waterscape. "The piece is a conscious effort on my part to combine my Eastern and Western cultural heritage—mixing my affinity for the southwestern Ohio terrain and its regional burial mounds with my love for the raked-sand gardens of Japan."

In a similar vein, Maya Lin went to the University of Michigan, in Ann Arbor, where on the north campus she created a landscape sculpture she called "Wave Field," located outside the university aerospace engineering building. Lin decided her artwork outside on the lawn should connect to what was going on inside the building, she sat down and talked with the scientists. They told her about their work and gave her some books on aerodynamics.

One book showed images of naturally repeating water waves, called stokes waves. This was it, she decided. This was her piece—a series of waves in the land. Lin went to work on her models, experimenting with the steepness of the curve of a wave and how to merge one wave into another to make the field look natural. She thought about how to mix the soil so everything would drain correctly. She didn't want puddles forming at the bottom of the waves. Then she presented her idea to the university engineers:

> They were going, "Well, that belongs over in naval engineering. It doesn't belong over here." . . . Scientists tend to get very specific and think you're gonna do it very literally. And I think art is about the non-literal connection. One thing doesn't correlate directly to the other, or it's too obvious. It's too easy and, in a way, if it can be understood and explained, it will not have its own life.

So Lin went ahead and created "Wave Field," a landscape of repetitive waves of water, sculpted out of earth. As she said of "Wave Field"—but it could be applied to a lot of her artwork—"What I'm trying to do is allow you to pay attention to beautiful forms in nature. I'm playing off of that, and I think it probably stems from the fundamental love I have of the natural landscape."

Maya Lin's Artistic Eye

Maya Lin continued to work in her New York studio, producing small-scale sculptures. She offered the public a view of these works in 1993, at the Wexner Center in Ohio, in a show called Public/Private. Then she assembled a more ambitious exhibition called Topologies, a collection of 15 sculptures in glass, wood, and wax, which was shown in a number of different cities, from New York to Houston, in 1997 and 1998. "For this show," she explained, "I made environmental works that were not meant for a specific site but would travel to museums and galleries across the country."

One piece in Topologies consisted of a huge pile of green-colored crushed safety glass. The work, called "Avalanche," is reminiscent of "Groundswell," the roof sculpture she created for the Wexner Center. There's a significant difference, however: Although "Groundswell" sits in Ann Arbor, Michigan (and isn't going anywhere), "Avalanche" gets transported from place to place. In addition, although "Avalanche" is smaller—only 14 tons (12.7 tonnes) of glass, compared to more than 40 tons (36.3 tonnes) for "Groundswell"—it's still a big, heavy pile of stuff to be moving all around the country!

Each time Lin moved the pile of broken glass, she swept it up and trucked it to the new location. Each time she unloaded the glass, she arranged the mound in a slightly different form, with slightly different slopes and curves—a little higher this time, a little broader the next. She would carefully rake the slope of the mound to create just the effect she was looking for. When it was dumped off in New York, at New York University, Lin piled up the mound against a glass wall, so the viewer could see into the back of the sculpture.

Another item from Topologies takes a look at typical topographic contours but from an unusual perspective. The piece is called "Topographic Landscape" and consists of long, thin wooden planks fastened together side by side, like the wooden floor of a house—except these wooden planks are bent and warped like a gently rolling field. The landscaped floor measures 16 feet (4.8 m) by 18 feet (5.5 m)—the size of a fairly large living room—and is based on computer-generated patterns made to look like an aerial view of natural hills. "All my art works deal with nature and the landscape," Lin explained. "And with that piece, some people think it looks like water waves. Other people think it's a sand dune."

The two large-scale sculptures, "Avalanche" and "Topographic Landscape," were exhibited with their smaller cousins—glass sculptures, landscape drawings, and wall-mounted works made of broken glass. To make the broken-glass pictures, Lin would drape a large plastic bag over a sheet of glass, then strike the edge of the glass with a hammer to shatter the pane. One example of this style, called "Flatlands," was made, according to Lin, "by breaking an inked plate of tempered glass then running it through a press, forming a set of unique impressions that are reminiscent of a map or an ice floe pattern."

THREE GEMS IN NEW YORK

Maya Lin has made New York City her home since 1987, and so it stands to reason that the New York cityscape would be sprinkled with her sculptures. Some of her works were produced for corporate offices and are for private eyes only, yet several significant works are open to the public.

Lin's ceiling sculpture "Eclipsed Time" marks a subterranean corner of Pennsylvania Station, near the ticket windows for Long Island Railroad. A huge wheel-shaped disk, housed in a 14-foot (4.3-meter) polished steel frame, inches back and forth across the hour marks, like the moon crossing over the sun in an eclipse. Soft backlighting in the ceiling illuminates the numbers, indicating the time in quarter-hour increments.

Lin said she hoped her clock would become a landmark where people could meet. "I know this is an old-fashioned notion," she said, "but all I really want is to hear people say, 'Meet me under the clock,' and then I'll be happy."

Farther downtown, on the edge of Chinatown, around the corner from Federal Courthouse Plaza, sits another Lin work:

A recent small-scale show called Systematic Landscapes debuted at the University of Washington in Seattle, in the summer of 2006. The focus of this show is on the natural world, as seen through a scientific lens. The centerpiece, called "2×4 Landscape," is made up of thousands of two-by-four-inch pieces of wood, all sloping upward to a height of 10 feet (3 meters). This sculpture is interactive—visitors can take off their shoes and climb to the 10-foot (3-m) summit.

Systematic Landscapes also includes a wire-mesh undersea landscape, and a 17-foot- (5.2-m-) high schematic of the Columbia River, made out of about 15,000 pushpins. "I am an artist who is focusing my attention on looking at the

"Sounding Stones," a row of four granite blocks from a quarry in Norway. Each of the massive gray blocks is about six feet (1.8 meters) square, with polished tops and rough-hewn sides. The granite blocks, according to Lin, are reminiscent of scholar's rocks—stones naturally shaped by water and valued for their contemplative nature in Chinese culture.

When the artwork was installed in 1996, water bubbled over the top and through the holes on the sides, creating a soothing gurgling sound. Since September 2001, however, the stones have been dry.

Chinatown is also the site of the Museum of Chinese in the Americas. The museum, founded in 1980, is housed on the second floor of an old school on Mulberry Street. Lin is refurbishing a seven-story brick building around the corner, though, and turning it into a state-of-the-art facility. The new museum, opening in 2007, will feature art exhibits and screening rooms and will also store thousands of records about the Chinese immigrant experience.

So next time you're in New York . . . see you under the clock!

natural world," she explained. "We now have different tools from the human eye to look at that world. A lot of what I do takes nature and in a way regurgitates it—through computers, through technology, the lens of these tools—then reintroduces it."

Even as Lin labored in her New York studio, creating interesting and unusual works, focusing on three-dimensional landscapes made of natural materials, the siren song of large-scale sculpture continued to call. One call that mattered, early on, came from the president of Yale University. He wanted to know: Could she do a sculpture to commemorate the women who had become part of the Yale community?

In her New York City studio in 1987, Maya Lin designs a 125-year-old mansion renovation and a competition for a large public sculpture.

Lin had spent seven years at Yale University—four as an undergraduate and three in the architectural graduate program—and she was eager to take on the task. First, she went to work on her research. Of course the school, founded in 1701, had historically been a male bastion. In the 1960s, however, the college, like a lot of other schools, transformed itself into a coeducational institution.

Lin also realized that women had populated the Yale campus long before they were officially allowed to enroll as undergraduates. In the 1800s, she found out, women called "silent listeners" were allowed to audit classes. Then, many of Yale's graduate schools, like the law, medical, and fine arts schools, went coed long before the undergraduate college.

However murky was the history of women at Yale, though, Lin knew that women were there to stay. She got an idea. "My first sketch was of a circular table and a spiral," she recalled. "A spiral has a beginning yet has no end, which is how I saw what this piece had to accomplish: It had to mark a time when women started at Yale, but it had to incorporate infinity and growth, with no end in the time line."

With that initial idea, Lin conceived "Women's Table," a large granite table that, like the Civil Rights Memorial, has a thin sheet of water streaming off the top. The spiral starts with a string of zeroes, demonstrating that there were no women at Yale for many years. "The first women that officially were enrolled were in the graduate school of art," she discovered. "Mr. Street, who donated the money to build the first art building, Street Hall, had two daughters. And his condition . . . was that his daughters would go there."

Lin asked the statistics department to determine the number of women attending the university for each year of the school's history. The art school, in 1873, enrolled 13 women, so that was her first positive number. Each year after that has a larger number. Although the numbers accurately reflect the enrollment figures, they more generally signify the emergence of women in American life.

The spiral ends with the date 1993, the year Maya Lin's "Women's Table" was dedicated. The year 1969 has a footnote, indicating that was the year the undergraduate college first admitted women. Because the spiral is an open design, it signifies the continuing influence of women at Yale, ongoing up to this day and to the years beyond. "And for once I was able to be a part of the piece," Lin noted. "As a Yale undergraduate and graduate student I am one of those numbers from 1977 to 1981 and from 1983 to 1986."

8

The Connection Is the Thing

Lin explains her view about the creative process, and how an artist gets her ideas:

> Everything you make is being made by every single experience you've ever had in your whole life, and on top of that, things you were born with. The true strength of the creative arts is that you allow yourself to think about something. Then how it finds its way in your mind to the surface through your hands . . . is intuited. There's reason to it. Could you formulate a mathematical theorem? Absolutely not.

Lin points out that she begins the process of designing a work by thinking about what emotional response she wants viewers to experience when they encounter her piece. In other words, she begins at the end: "I begin by imagining an artwork verbally. I try to describe in writing what the project is, what it is trying to do. I need to understand the artwork without giving it a specific materiality or solid form. I try not to find the form too soon. Instead I try to think about it as an idea without a shape."

Lin typically writes down what she is feeling about a piece and what she wants other people to experience emotionally when they see her work—as she was required to do for the Vietnam Veterans Memorial competition so many years ago. Sometimes, the purpose of the project is very clear to her. With the Vietnam Veterans Memorial, she recalled:

> I needed to ask myself the question 'What is the purpose of a war memorial at the close of the 20th century?' My question led me to study war memorials, from the earliest funereal stelae to the monuments of the great world wars. I felt that the design should focus on the individuals who died and not the politics surrounding that war. I sought a design that would bring the viewer to an honest acceptance of the deaths of those individuals.

After thinking about a project and writing down her feelings, she begins her process of research—as she researched funerary architecture for the Vietnam Veterans Memorial, and the civil rights movement for her Montgomery memorial, and the history of women at Yale for "Women's Table."

"I always research something for three months, a year, six months. I think I do it because it's an incubation period," she explains. "And it's also because I come from a family of academics. And I guess I miss school. So, this is my way of being a little bit of a student."

Lin admits that she never becomes an expert. She didn't select the names for the Vietnam Veterans Memorial. The U.S. Department of Defense did that. She didn't pick the events for the Civil Rights Memorial, or choose the numbers for "Women's

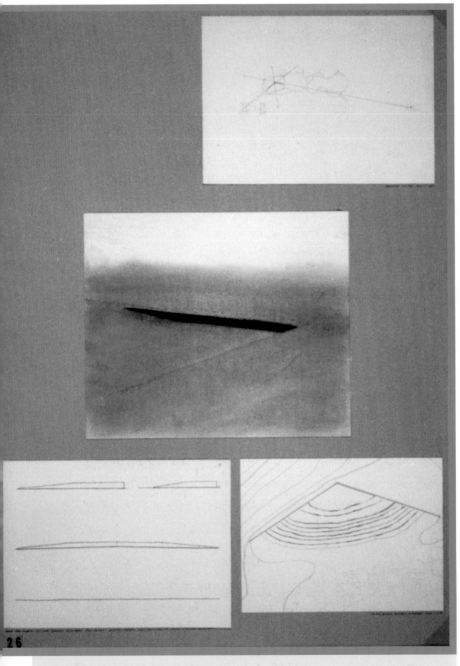

Maya Lin's competition drawings of the Vietnam Veterans Memorial show how she envisioned the piece would appear within the landscape. Lin researches each project for months before designing it.

Being Asian American   DAUGHER OF IMMIGRANTS

When Lin was growing up, her parents never really talked about the past, about their lives in China. Maya never knew her grandparents or any of her aunts or uncles. She was 21, a college graduate, before her father told her about her aunt Lin Hui-yin or anything else about her influential ancestors in China.

Like many first-generation American children, Maya was not particularly interested in her parents' native country. She did not learn how to speak Chinese, or exhibit any interest in Chinese history or current political affairs in the Far East.

Even as a child, though, Maya couldn't help but feel that her family was somehow different. By leaving China and settling in the United States, her parents felt separated from their past, yet somehow isolated from the rest of America. That may, at least in part, explain why Maya did not fit into the typical American teenage experience in Athens, Ohio.

Maya's ancestors were Chinese. Her parents were Chinese, bringing with them to America a worldview rooted in Chinese and Taoist philosophy. Maya herself, as she explains in her book, lives on a sort of boundary—on the line between East and West. Reporter Phil McCombs, after Lin won the Vietnam Veterans Memorial competition, said, "Maya Lin is an American girl from the Midwest, but she is Chinese in her bones."

Lin's future, however, is America. She explained that although she could easily be categorized as Chinese American, she identifies herself as American and believes in the American dream. "To me the American dream is being able to follow your own personal calling. And to be able to do what you want is an incredible freedom that we have. . . . [But] the American dream also represents a responsibility to share it, and to not just hoard the freedom, but share with other countries and with people in our own country."

Table." Nevertheless, while she's working on a piece, she can become immersed in her subject. Sometimes, too, she might give it a rest for a while, going on to something else, filing what she knows in the back of her mind.

"I try to let ideas percolate to the surface, not to force them," she says. "It might take me two or three years to develop an artwork. I try not to come up with one construct and then make the art around it, an approach encouraged in most architectural schools. I am interested in letting the process of making the work control it. . . . I think of all my work, be it a building or a sculpture, as art conceived intuitively."

Although she's careful not to force a design, or leap to any conclusion, eventually, one day, an idea comes to her. It could happen when she visits a site; it could happen while she's reading, or even sleeping. "I do not see this process as being under my conscious control," she admits. "It is a process of percolation, with the form eventually finding its way to the surface."

The idea for her design typically arrives in her head fully formed—like an egg, she says, that suddenly appears at her doorstep. "Generally, the first concept, the initial idea, I can just wake up one morning after having not worked on it for a year, get up, do a sketch, make a model, and I know that's what it is."

Most architects sketch out their designs on paper, but Lin thinks in three dimensions and prefers working with a model. "I was never drawn to two-dimensional processes but always to three-dimensional arts: sculpture, metalsmithing, anything I could physically work with my hands. . . . I think with my hands."

Once she has that idea modeled in clay—or mashed potatoes—she tries to remain true to her original concept. She feels that the challenge in building a project is to avoid the temptation to constantly revise it as she goes along, trying to make it better or more refined. Instead, she tries to stay focused on her original vision. She tries to make her final work resemble that original "egg" as much as possible.

Lin makes a concerted effort not to rush an idea. She deliberately goes slowly to arrive at her image. Once she gets it, though, she sticks to it. She says, "Unlike someone who has an idea and then works it and works it and polishes it, once I get this idea, it's quick, and it's pretty pure. The idea is to keep it clean. And usually I don't embellish, I don't add that much."

Her objective is to create a bond with the person who looks at her art, to forge a personal connection. Whether her project is large or small, her goal is to give the viewer an opportunity to think about things—sometimes within a context of history, relying on memory to make an impact.

At the Vietnam Veterans Memorial, for example, visitors make a passage through the time frame of the Vietnam War. And as they walk along the wall, seeing their reflection against the black granite, they feel their connection to the war and the people involved in that disruptive period of history.

Both the Civil Rights Memorial and the "Women's Table" rely on water to engage the viewers. People touch the water and create ripples—interacting with the work. Other works, such as "Wave Field" and "2×4 Landscape" invite the viewer to walk—or climb—through the piece in order to participate and become part of the art.

"I try to think of my work as creating a private conversation with each person," she says, perhaps hoping her audience will experience some of her own journey. She says she attempts to provide for the viewer "passages of awareness, to what my mother would describe in Taoism as 'the Way': an introspective and personal searching."

Lin's larger works also create for the visitor a special physical place. The landscape becomes a part of the piece. "A strong respect and love for the land exists throughout my work," she

An overview of the crowds that gathered around the Vietnam Veterans Memorial during the dedication on the National Mall in Washington, D.C., on Saturday, November 13, 1982, shows the connection Maya Lin strives for between visitor and memorial.

explains. "I cannot remember a time when I was not concerned with environmental issues or when I did not feel humbled by the beauty of the natural world."

Lin uses the landscape to her advantage; she incorporates it into her work. She has pointed out that Western architecture creates buildings that separate man from nature, that try to establish man's domination over nature. She prefers the Eastern approach—working within the context of nature, creating buildings that fit into the existing landscape.

Going back to her high-school days, Lin is also a student of science. Consequently, her view of nature is not romantic or melodramatic. She does not shy away from scientific methods to help her imagine and create her Earth-inspired sculptures. Lin will consider satellite-based photography or consult computer-aided imaging to help her view the Earth in a different way. She'll employ the principles of fluid dynamics or study topographic mapping to help her create perspective.

There's also the practical side, the technical side, of architecture. Lin will first create her designs and elaborate on them, and when necessary present them to her clients. She will then go back and work up specific drawings and models, all made to scale, to provide a blueprint for her work. That involves all the nuts and bolts of construction, "all the little finicky things—the thickness of paving stones, stairway tread dimensions, asking a lot of technical, structural questions, coordinating with an engineer. You're really figuring out all the dimensions you need to know to get something built."

Lin uses math and geology to create her own unique vision of nature. She also draws strength from the natural world. What inspires her? She forms her vision from all things in nature and the world around her, from the rock formations below the earth, to the stars above it. She says, "I think what my work is about is appreciating and being respectful of nature, which ties into an inherent love for the natural environment.

I will go to sites that are just so beautiful beyond compare. I know that nothing I do can ever be better than what this planet, what this land, what the natural resources, what this place is."

9

Journey of Discovery

Maya Lin currently lives in New York City with her husband, Daniel Wolf, an art dealer and art collector. Married in 1996, the couple has two daughters, India and Rachel, who, according to Lin, appear Caucasian. Yet, unlike their mother, the two girls have taken Chinese lessons.

Maya met her husband while on vacation in Colorado, and they later got engaged during a camping trip. Now the family lives in New York, but they have a vacation house in Ridgway, Colorado, where they spend time in the summer.

So Lin continues to live between two worlds. "It's a funny place to be," she says, "but it's also who you are. You might try to understand it. And I think at this point I try to embrace it; it's great. You can share a culture and take from both, but it's a balancing act."

She also continues to live in the world between art and architecture. She designed a line of furniture for Knoll, an office furniture manufacturer, in 1998, to mark the company's sixtieth anniversary. Called The Maya Lin Collection: The Earth

Maya Lin's line of stone furniture is produced by Knoll, Inc.

Is Not Flat, it features furniture with undulating surfaces of arcs and curves.

A series of stools made from concrete and fiberglass, called "Stones," was influenced by her husband's collection of pre-

THE TWIN TOWERS

Maya Lin was in Colorado on September 11, 2001, when two jet-liners hit the World Trade Center, only a few blocks south of her studio. That morning, Lin phoned her brother Tan, who watched the fiery crash from his Manhattan apartment. Lin and her husband returned to New York as soon as they could.

When the *New York Times* asked a group of experts for ideas on how to rebuild downtown, Lin offered some sketches. She suggested building an artificial island in the Hudson River to memorialize the event, with a walkway leading to the site of the World Trade Center. She also mused about placing twin reflecting pools at the base of the World Trade Center to mark the footprint of the collapsed towers.

In 2002, the Lower Manhattan Development Corporation—an organization created to take responsibility for reconstructing the site—solicited proposals to rebuild the towers. The winning design called for five office buildings to replace the Twin Towers. The tallest of the five, the Freedom Tower, would spiral up a symbolic 1776 feet. The plan, which also envisions a new transit station, a museum, and an underground memorial for those who were killed.

Meanwhile, a separate competition was held to design a memorial to the victims. In April 2003, a jury of 13 people was selected to judge the contest. Lin agreed to sit on the jury.

A young New Yorker named Michael Arad, was announced the winner from a pool of 5,000 entries. Arad's submission was called "Reflecting Absence" and features two reflecting pools marking the footprint of the towers, placed 30 feet (9 m) underground, framed by cascading waterfalls and the names of almost 3,000 victims.

Columbian art. More generally, Lin said she was inspired on her honeymoon in the South Pacific. "On my honeymoon, I spent a lot of time looking out at the ocean and trying to see and understand the Earth's curve."

She also spent time designing houses. The Weber residence, in Williamstown, Massachusetts, is centered around a rock garden. The roof rises and dips to mimic the hills in the distance. In 1999, she redesigned the New York City apartment of Internet millionaire Peter Norton. There are skylights and frosted-glass walls, and sliding doors inspired by Japanese homes. Concealed storage spaces, disappearing walls, and hidden cabinets complete the puzzle. "Minimalism was never so much fun," enthused the *New York Times* in its coverage of the unveiling of the apartment.

She later expanded her architectural horizons to Colorado and California. A 2006 house in Colorado was inspired by Asian puzzle boxes, with sliding doors and boxes within boxes. One cube forms the main house; a second cube contains the garage, a home gym, and guest quarters. The two main sections are connected by a second-story deck. Located on a ranch in the Rockies, the house is settled into a low mesa, with views of the mountains framed in every window.

Lin has also designed corporate offices, museums, and even some more functional structures, like a garbage plant in the Bronx and a bakery in a downtrodden section of Yonkers, New York. She designed a library for the Children's Defense Fund, an organization dedicated to helping underprivileged children.

The Children's Defense Fund acquired the Tennessee farm of Alex Haley (author of *Roots*) after he died in 1992. The board of directors turned the Haley farm into a conference center; it also is used for a summer camp for high-school and college students. In developing the site, they approached Lin and asked her to build a library.

On the property, Lin found an abandoned wooden barn, built in the 1860s. It was a typical example of what is known as a Tennessee cantilevered barn—a standard barn perched on top of two rough-hewn animal cribs. The raised floor of the barn originally protected the grain from flooding, while it also provided a shaded area for the animals.

Lin took the building apart, supported it with a new foundation and a steel skeleton structure, and put it back together again. Although the outside of the building looks rustic and old-fashioned, the inside is a modern version of a one-room schoolhouse. Light wood walls and maple floors frame the high-ceilinged main reading room. A large picture window offers views of the surrounding hillside. Down below, splinters of light shine between the logs into the lower cribs. One of the old cribs has been transformed into a gift shop, while the other houses the stairs leading up to the main room. In between the cribs, Lin installed a Japanese-style granite fountain to grace the open-air entrance.

A couple of years later, Lin went back to the farm to work on an interfaith chapel, located across a pond from the library, next to an apple orchard. She envisioned a wooden structure, about the size of a large house, which would seat about 200 people. She wrapped the outside of the chapel in locally grown cypress, with no windows, so the building looks like a big boat sitting in an open field.

Lin cut several skylights into the chapel roof, to let in plenty of natural light. She made the wall at the back of the chapel retractable. It opens up to provide an outdoor pavilion that can accommodate an overflow crowd. Inside the chapel there are no pews, just chairs that can be arranged in various configurations, depending on the occasion.

Lin's world was expanding and began to seem limitless. She was building houses and sculptures, furniture and factories, libraries and churches. Although she was based in New York City, her work extended to Pennsylvania and Ohio, Alabama

The Langston Hughes Library at CDF Haley Farms in Tennessee was created by Maya Lin through a donation by Barnes and Noble chairman Len Riggio and his wife, Louise.

and North Carolina, and Tennessee. Her next commission was another assignment in Michigan.

Officials from the city of Grand Rapids wanted to make the downtown area of this state's second-largest city more attractive, starting with a 3½-acre (1.4 hectares) central square. They contacted Lin. She was interested in the project, but only if her artwork would provide a catalyst to renovate the tough urban area and bring life to the city. "What I wanted to do was take the idea of sculpture and grow it into a park," she said.

She envisioned what she called an experiential park with an amphitheater that would seat 1,500 people, along with a pond, a fountain, and a skating rink. The theme of the park would focus on water, harking back to the original great rapids—rapids that long ago were taken out to improve a flooding problem.

Her park would feature water in its three familiar physical stages—solid, liquid, and gas. According to Lin, the water would "bring conceptually to the heart of Grand Rapids a park that refers back to the rapids for which the city was named. Water becomes a metaphor for the design—like an undercurrent that flows throughout."

It took a couple of years to raise the money and get all the approvals—the park was finally dedicated in the summer of 2001—but eventually the plan was set. Lin installed the amphitheater and the skating rink. A simple pool represents liquid. A fountain sprays out a ring of mist, signifying vapor. Finally, the skating ring itself presents the solid form of water.

The Riggio-Lynch Interfaith Chapel at CDF Haley Farms.

Maya Lin at the site of her installation project in downtown Grand Rapids, Michigan, where she has created an ice skating rink lit from below with fiber optics to resemble a night sky.

Lin embedded a series of lights in the concrete base. They would shine up through the ice in the winter. In the summer, when the ice was gone, the lights would decorate an outdoor dance floor used at summer concerts. She arranged the floor lights to mimic the night sky over Grand Rapids on the millennium: January 1, 2000.

10

Go West, Young Woman

L in placed her first sculpture on the West Coast, a piece called "Timetable," on the campus of Stanford University in California. It was dedicated in October 2000 to mark the seventy-fifth anniversary of the school of engineering. The eight-ton black granite sculpture serves as a working clock, with rings and disks and rotating parts that mark time by revolving once every minute, once an hour, and once a year.

Like several other Lin works, "Timetable" uses water, which wells up from the center and spills over the sides. "I've always just thought about it as water percolating up through the earth, like a spring," Lin said. "Now it's obvious to me that everything has a geologic implication."

Lin has always felt comfortable on a college campus. She was to do another West Coast campus sculpture, at the University of California, Irvine. It was an outdoor arts plaza linking two theaters and an art gallery.

First, though, she went back home to create an earthwork installation in her hometown of Athens, Ohio. Called "Input,"

Maya Lin worked in tandem with her brother, Tan, to create a "landscape of words" for the Bicentennial Park that reflects their shared memories of Athens, Ohio. Cutting the ribbon in May 2004 are Ohio University President Robert Glidden *(left)*, Rachel Wolf, Maya Lin, India Wolf, Tan Lin and university vice-president John Kotowski. Rachel, then 4, and India, 6, are Maya Lin's daughters.

it looks like a giant computer punch card carved into an old football field. The piece, created for Ohio University's bicentennial celebration has a personal side for Lin. When she was in high school, she studied programming at the college, and she remembered struggling mightily with those early computer cards.

Meanwhile, Lin was working on the Irvine project, which took almost five years. It was interrupted by the September 11, 2001, tragedy that took place only a few blocks from her Manhattan studio. After September 11, she found it difficult to work.

She was also stymied by the Irvine project. She knew her plaza needed a water table, but what should it look like? She had trouble visualizing the design. She says of this time:

> What was hardest for me was what the text on the water table would be. I experimented with different texts, dance language, musical notation, but nothing worked for me. Then one day, while I was doodling at a meeting, there it was: A single curving line was the result. It took me 2½ years to come up with that. The rest was easy. After all, I'm a campus brat . . . so it feels like home turf to me. I love working on college campuses. You have a very engaged, very active audience.

The centerpiece of the University of California, Irvine, project is a gravel rectangle, punctuated with seven granite benches. The benches face the water table, marked by a gentle curve, which represents both the performing and visual arts. A nearby wall is surfaced with tiny glass beads that form a rectangle. It looks something like the blank screen of a drive-in movie. That's no coincidence; her white wall doubles as an outdoor theater screen.

Now that she was on the West Coast, Lin got involved in another project—not on a college campus, but across a whole state. Although Lin hadn't wanted to be typecast as a builder of monuments, she did want to make one more memorial—one that would focus on the extinction of species, envisioning a series of markers that would monitor the health of the planet.

In the meantime, though, Lin's sense of history, and her understanding of the emotional significance of major events—as well as her inevitable desire to make a big statement—would lead her to commemorate a great historical turning point, the opening of the American West.

In 1999, a number of nonprofit organizations in the Pacific Northwest got together to decide how to mark the upcoming bicentennial of the Lewis and Clark expedition—a voyage that changed America.

Meriwether Lewis and William Clark, along with about 30 compatriots, set out from St. Louis in the spring of 1804 to explore the vast lands acquired by President Thomas Jefferson in the Louisiana Purchase. The group, called the Corps of Discovery, paddled up the Missouri River, struggled over the Rocky Mountains, then followed the westward-flowing rivers to the Pacific Ocean. They arrived at the Pacific in November 1805. They wintered over on the coast, and returned to St. Louis in September 1806, bringing back reports of the rivers and mountains, the flora and fauna, and the Native Americans they met along the way.

Now, 200 years later, civic groups and Native American leaders launched the Confluence Project to mark the route of Lewis and Clark along the Columbia River and its tributaries. They felt that the notion of confluence—the idea of flowing together—would symbolize the meeting of two great cultures in the Northwest: the Native Americans, who were already there, and the European Americans, who were on their way.

The organizers of the Confluence Project thought about how to commemorate this complicated historical event. Lewis and Clark's explorations advanced scientific knowledge and opened the American West, but they also brought disease and death to Native Americans and destruction to the natural environment. As organizers contemplated the complexities of the moment, they gravitated toward Maya Lin, the artist who so eloquently captured the conflicting emotions of the Vietnam War. In 1999, representatives of the Confluence Project approached Maya Lin. Could she take on this assignment?

Lin said no. She did not want to make any more memorials or monuments. The Confluence Project committee was persistent, however. It turned to the then-governor of Washington for help. Governor Gary Locke, who not only shared a Chinese heritage with Lin, but was also a graduate of Yale University. He wrote Lin a letter. She did not respond.

Then one day in 2000, David DiCesare, an active member of the Confluence Project, was in New York to attend a wedding. He decided to take a chance and stop in, unannounced, at Lin's studio. He knocked on the door and was invited in by an assistant. Lin suddenly appeared in the doorway. She listened to his presentation. Tea was served. Lin listened some more and began to understand the significance of the Confluence Project and the challenge it would present to her.

With some further encouragement from her fans in the Northwest—including Governor Locke—Lin finally agreed to produce a series of memorials for the project. No one knew at that point what the artworks would look like, but all agreed they would be placed at various locations along the route of Lewis and Clark on their journey to the Pacific.

In 2000, when the project began, the commemoration was slated to be a $12 million undertaking. Soon, however, the project expanded to include the renovation of parks, the refurbishing of waterfronts, and the restoration of historical landmarks. Before it was fully realized, the Confluence Project was to become a $25 million megamemorial. Lin, who originally agreed to do four sculptures, would sign on for seven. For her labors, she would be paid $1 million. Before it's over, she will have been working on the project for 10 years.

Lin agreed with the members of the Confluence Project that her artwork should offer history lessons, pay respect to the native cultures, and also restore some of the landscape to a more natural condition. "I'm a very committed environmentalist," said Lin. "I want to reflect back on Lewis and Clark not just from a cultural history of the Native American tribes, but also from the great ecological, environmental changes that have shifted in the last 200 years."

Lin flew out to Oregon and Washington on several scouting trips. She explored potential sites, taking photographs,

SEVEN SITES ON THE COLUMBIA

1. **Chief Timothy Park, near Clarkston, Washington.** In 1805, Lewis and Clark met a group of Nez Perce at the confluence of two rivers, the Clearwater and the Snake, who welcomed them and gave them directions. (Chief Timothy Park is named after a Nez Perce chief who was friendly to the settlers.) On this site, Lin is creating an amphitheater using stones etched with verses describing stories of the Nez Perce.

2. **Sacajawea State Park, Pasco, Washington.** The park is named after the Native American girl who guided the Corps of Discovery through the mountains. Lin envisions two pieces to signify the two cultures: a dock engraved with excerpts from the Lewis and Clark journals and a table showing the directions from which the various tribes once gathered here to trade.

3. **Celilo Falls, east of The Dalles, Oregon.** Lewis and Clark had to portage their boats around the Celilo Falls of the Columbia, once a traditional Native American fishing ground. Lin's plan is to clear a path descending underground to the river, where a glass wall will offer an underwater aquarium-like view facing the original falls, now buried underwater behind the Bonneville Dam.

4. **Sandy River, near Troutdale, Oregon.** Lewis and Clark complained that the area was so crowded with birds that the explorers couldn't sleep. Lin plans to build a bird-watching station listing the 102 species of birds that Lewis and Clark observed, many of them never before known to science. She will also note the status of the species today—whether the species is extinct, endangered, or healthy.

5. **Land Bridge, Fort Vancouver National Historic Site, Vancouver, Washington.** Lin is building the 40-foot- (12.2-m-) wide bridge that vaults over the highway and contains a meandering walking path bordered by flowers and shrubs.

(continues)

(continued)

6. **Frenchman's Bar Park, Vancouver, Washington.** The site, across the Columbia from where the Willamette enters the river, marks the homeland of the Chinook Nation. Lin plans a landscape design, perhaps in conjunction with an air and water research station to be used by several universities in Washington and Oregon.
7. **Cape Disappointment State Park, Ilwaco, Washington.** Located at the mouth of the Columbia, this windy beach marks the spot where Lewis and Clark first spied the Pacific Ocean. Lin has restored the land to its natural environment and installed her artworks connecting the bay to the Pacific Ocean.

making notes, generating ideas. She also invited members of the Confluence Project, as well as people from the Chinook, Umatilla, and Nez Perce tribes, to visit her New York studio to offer their views.

After endless discussions and bureaucratic complications—and a major fundraising effort—the Confluence Project finally settled on the seven sites where Lin would tell the story of Lewis and Clark. Seven works at seven different sites, but according to Lin herself, they were conceived as a single work, connected by the mighty Columbia River.

On April 30, 2005, Lin traveled from New York to the state of Washington, to attend a tribal blessing. The event occurred outside of Clarkston, Washington, the site of the most eastern of Lin's monuments, near the Idaho border. On a clear sunny day, she spoke to a group of about 120 people, including tribal members, state officials, teachers, and donors. They sat on folding chairs at Chief Timothy Park, on an island in the Snake River. She told them how she wanted to commemorate Lewis and Clark and the Corps of Discovery. She also told them how she wanted to honor the Native Americans who were here before them and to make people aware of the environment and how it has been changed in 200 years.

"I am a very deeply committed environmentalist," Lin said. She continued:

> I think the Columbia River and its tributaries formed probably one of the most abundant life streams ever, and in just 200 years, where are we today? Now . . . I would like to predict that 200 years from now, we might be heading in a better place. And that does not mean some kind of romantic ideal about returning to something pristine. But it does mean . . . we can learn to live better with the environment.

She noted that she was commissioned to create seven works along a 450-mile stretch of the Columbia River and its tributaries. "I see it as one river, one life blood of a system," she said. She went on to ask, "Where is God's country? God's country is here, in places like this. It's pretty special."

A Umatilla tribal leader recalled the 1855 treaty that turned over some 6.4 million acres of Native American land to the United States. A Nez Perce rang a bell and spoke of peace. "For a long time people lived in peace on this land. Every morning as soon as they woke up, they thanked the Creator."

The tribal leaders continued their ceremony amid the calls of seagulls circling above the river. Lin stood at the edge of a natural basin on the island. Nez Perce drummers played songs, and blessings were offered into the brisk gusts of wind that blew down the river.

After the ceremony, Lin walked through the grass and the wildflowers. "What we just witnessed today, I feel an incredible responsibility," she mused. "This place has power. For me, it's about the land. For them, it's the Creator. For everyone, it's something."

A few months later, in November 2005, Lin was back again in Washington State. She would take part, together with fellow architect Johnpaul Jones, in the groundbreaking ceremony for one of the monuments. It was a land bridge near Fort Vancouver, scheduled to be completed by the end of 2007.

Fort Vancouver stood as the most important settlement in the Northwest during the first half of the nineteenth century. The spot was also the terminus of an ancient Native American trail, called the Klickitat Trail, which ran from Puget Sound South to the Columbia River. In the late nineteenth century, however, the railroad came through Vancouver, and the city was cut off from the riverfront. Later, a highway was built along the river, as well.

As part of the Confluence Project, Lin conceived of a bridge that would arc over the highway and connect modern-day Vancouver with the old riverfront. Lin enlisted the help of Jeanpaul Jones, of the Seattle architectural firm Jones & Jones, and together they envisioned a 40-foot- (12.2-m-) wide bridge vaulting about 700 feet (213.4 m) over the highway. The bridge would contain a meandering path for pedestrians and bicycles, but no cars. The rest of the structure would be planted with native grasses, flowers, and shrubs.

"We just grabbed the prairie landscape and dragged it over to the river. It is reestablishing the land back to the way it once was," explained Johnpaul Jones, who is half Native American, half Welsh. Jones is also the architect for the Smithsonian's National Museum of the American Indian, in Washington, D.C.

At the groundbreaking ceremony for the Vancouver footbridge, Lin said, "I see it as kind of like the St. Louis Gateway Arch." The half-moon-shaped bridge would span the highway and connect the city to the river for the first time in a century.

The very next day, November 18, 2005, the day that marked the two-hundredth anniversary of the arrival of Lewis and Clark at the Pacific Ocean, Lin made her way out to Cape Disappointment, where the Columbia River roils into the Pacific. This windy beach marks the spot where Lewis and Clark first spied the Pacific Ocean—the culmination of their long and arduous journey.

Lin was there for the dedication of the first of her seven artworks completed for the Confluence Project—an installation that includes an amphitheater, an estuary-viewing platform, a fish-cleaning basin, a totem-pole forest, and a network of trails connecting them all. Lin spoke to an assembled group of civic leaders and Chinook tribal members in dedicating the still-not-quite-finished work. Speaking of the totem-pole forest, she said, "I see it as a sacred cedar circle, because it is the sacred wood of the Chinook tribes. . . and I think I'm doing this in honor of their presence here."

A 16-foot- (4.9-m-) long chunk of columnar basalt, weighing some 12 tons (10.9 t), lay on its side. Words relating an ancient Chinook creation myth were carved on the basalt. The words described how a big fish was cut up in the wrong way. The fish was transformed into a giant thunderbird, and the thunderbird laid the eggs that became human beings. This 12-ton rock would be part of a working fish-cleaning station, near a boat dock in the bay. The basalt would have a big sink, with a hose and running water, so fisherman could gut and clean their fish.

"You're not coming here to see what I've done," she explained, visualizing her sculpture in use. "You're coming here because you've always come here, because you've just caught a king salmon that's two and a half feet long, and you're going to cut your fish here. And then, maybe, you're going to start reading this and you're going to say, 'What is going on here?' And maybe you'll get a hint that this was the sacred grounds of the Chinook tribe."

She pointed to the trail and spoke about how it would demonstrate for visitors the fragility of the environment and importance of this site, where the fresh waters from the Rockies mix with the saltwater of the Pacific. At the end of the trail sat a 6-foot-wide, 9-inch (1.8-m-wide, 23-cm) -tall panel of stainless

Maya Lin stands in front of a fish-cleaning table following its dedication in 2005 in Cape Disappointment, Washington, the first of seven Columbia River projects.

steel. It was one of six panels to be installed along a path leading to the ocean. The panels would feature entries from the Lewis and Clark journals, marking the progress of their expedition to the Pacific. On the viewing platform, a November 15, 1805, entry from one of the expedition members reads: "This morning weather appeared to settle and clear off but the river remains still rough. . . . Went about 3 miles when we came to the mouth of the river where it empties into a handsome bay."

A separate walkway made out of crushed oyster shells would lead to a quiet glade, where people could reflect on the expedition and its effects on the environment and the Native Americans.

There would be an overlook and a small outdoor public amphitheater, which was nearly complete. Next to the amphitheater would stand a totem of six upright cedar trunks found washed up on the beach, surrounding a central cedar stump placed on the oyster shells. They would represent the seven points on the Native American compass: north, south, east, west, up, down, and in.

"In all these places, I'm moving the viewer to the boundary," Lin explained. "To the boundary of the water and the land, the forest and meadow—looking to find a new connection to the natural world around us."

Lin has completed many projects, but she has long had a particular dream. She wrote in her book *Boundaries*, "There is one last memorial I would like to create. This memorial would focus on the most important issue for me while growing up and to this day: the environment and man's relationship to it." She envisioned this memorial not as a singular monument, but a series of markers existing in many places, all monitoring the environmental health of the planet: a memorial to the extinction of the species.

Maybe Lin has already done this in her Confluence Project and the seven memorials linking exploration and the environment. Lin has miles to go before she sleeps, however, and one thing is for sure: She will surprise us once again with her creativity, her daring, and her vision of the past and the future.

CHRONOLOGY

1948–1949 Maya Lin's father, Henry Lin, emigrates to the United States; her mother, Julia Chang, flees Shanghai as Communists bomb the city.

1951 Julia Chang graduates from Smith College and meets Henry Lin at the University of Washington, in Seattle, while doing graduate work.

TIMELINE

Fall 1983
Lin enrolls in master's program at Yale School of Architecture.

1996
Lin marries art dealer and collector Daniel Wolf.

March 1981
Lin wins Vietnam Veterans Memorial design competition.

November 5, 1989
Civil Rights Memorial is dedicated in Montgomery, Alabama.

1959

1996

October 9, 1959
Maya Lin is born in Athens, Ohio.

Fall 1993
"Women's Table" is dedicated at Yale University; Lin builds "Groundswell" at Ohio State University.

1977
Lin enrolls at Yale University in New Haven, Connecticut.

1986
Lin graduates from Yale with M.S. in Architecture.

1956 Maya's older brother, Tan Lin, is born.

1959 *October 9* Maya Lin is born in Athens, Ohio.

1977 Maya enrolls at Yale University in New Haven, Connecticut.

1981 *March* She submits design for Vietnam Veterans Memorial.

1981 *May* Maya Lin wins competition; graduates from Yale University; moves to Washington, D.C.

1981–1982 Lin works as consultant on Vietnam Veterans Memorial.

1982 *Fall* Lin moves to Boston, enrolls at Harvard, drops out, and goes to work for Boston

Fall 1998
Topologies tours in five cities across America; Lin produces line of furniture for Knoll.

2000
Lin publishes autobiographical *Boundaries*; takes on the Confluence Project to commemorate the Lewis and Clark expedition.

April 2006
Artwork is dedicated at Cape Disappointment.

Summer 2006
Maya Lin: Systematic Landscapes opens in Seattle.

2008 (projected)
Lin finishes the Confluence Project.

1998

2007

1999
Lin builds park for Grand Rapids, Michigan; finishes Langston Hughes Library at the Children Defense Fund's Haley Farm in Tennessee.

2002–2004
Lin serves on jury for World Trade Center memorial competition.

2007 (projected)
Lin renovates New York building for the Museum of Chinese in the Americas.

architectural firm; attends dedication of Vietnam Veterans Memorial in Washington, D.C.

1983 *Fall* Maya Lin enrolls in master's program at Yale School of Architecture.

1986 Lin graduates from Yale with M.S. in Architecture.

1987 *November* Lin opens studio in New York City; is awarded honorary doctor's degree from Yale University.

1989 Civil Rights Memorial is dedicated in Montgomery, Alabama.

1993 *Fall* "Women's Table" is dedicated at Yale University; Lin builds "Groundswell" at Ohio State University.

1994 Lin designs "Eclipsed Time" for Pennsylvania Station in New York City; installs "Wave Field" at University of Michigan.

1996 Lin marries art dealer and collector Daniel Wolf.

1998 Topologies tours in five cities across America; Lin produces line of furniture for Knoll.

1999 Lin builds park for Grand Rapids, Michigan; finishes Langston Hughes Library at the Children Defense Fund's Haley Farm in Tennessee.

2000 Lin publishes autobiographical *Boundaries* to explain and summarize her work up to that time; agrees to take on the Confluence Project, a series of memorials commemorating the Lewis and Clark expedition.

2000 *October* Lin dedicates "Timetable" at Stanford University, her first artwork on the West Coast.

2001 *September 11* New York's World Trade Center is attacked, only a few blocks from Maya Lin's studio.

2002–2004 Lin serves on jury for World Trade Center memorial competition.

2004 *July* Interfaith chapel is dedicated at Children Defense Fund's Haley Farm in Tennessee.

2005 *October* Unveiling of Maya Lin–designed "Arts Plaza" at University of California, Irvine.

2006 *April* Artwork dedicated at Cape Disappointment, the first of the Confluence Project pieces to be completed.

2006 *Summer* Maya Lin: Systematic Landscapes opens in Seattle.

2007 *(projected)* Lin renovates New York building for the Museum of Chinese in the Americas.

2008 *(projected)* Maya Lin finishes the Confluence Project.

GLOSSARY

abstract—Artistic imagery that is not concrete; it does not accurately represent a material object—more theoretical than practical.

basalt—A dark, dense volcanic rock.

berm—A ledge or shoulder, especially along the side of a road.

estuary—An inlet from the sea, especially at the mouth of a river where the tide meets the current.

funerary—Of or relating to burial.

geode—A circular stone with a cavity lined with inward growing crystals.

granite—A hard igneous rock formed from cooling lava, consisting mostly of mica and quartz.

immigrant—One who comes to a new country.

memorial—Anything created to help people remember a person or event.

minimalist—A modern art style that stresses the notion of reducing an artwork to the fewest shapes, colors, and lines, without trying to accurately represent a material object.

monument—A building or sculpture built to remember or honor a person or event.

obelisk—A tall four-sided shaft of stone that usually tapers toward the top.

stela (pl. stelae)—An upright stone slab or pillar, usually engraved with artwork or an inscription and used as a grave or monument, especially by ancient Greeks and Egyptians.

Taoism—A Chinese religion or philosophy based on the doctrines of Lao Tse advocating simplicity and selflessness.

BIBLIOGRAPHY

BOOKS

Ashabranner, Brent. *Always to Remember: The Story of the Vietnam Veterans Memorial*. New York: G.P. Putnam's Sons, 1988.

Bowdish, Lynea. *With Courage: Seven Women Who Changed America*. New York: Mondo Publishing, 2004.

Italia, Bob. *Maya Lin: Honoring Our Forgotten Heroes*. Edina, Minn.: Abdo & Daughters, 1993.

Lin, Maya. *Boundaries*. New York: Simon & Schuster, 2000.

Malone, Mary. *Maya Lin: Architect and Artist*. Springfield, N.J.: Enslow Publishers, 1995.

Ou-fan Lee, Leo. *The Romantic Generation of Modern Chinese Writers*. Cambridge, Mass.: Harvard University Press, 1973.

Scruggs, Jan C., and Joel L. Swerdlow. *To Heal a Nation: The Vietnam Veterans Memorial*. New York: Harper & Row, 1985.

Sollins, Susan, et al. *Art 21: Art in the Twenty-first Century,* vol. 1. New York: Harry N. Abrams, 2001.

Spence, Jonathan D. *Gate of Heavenly Peace: The Chinese Revolution 1985–1980*. New York: Viking Press, 1981.

PERIODICALS

Allen, Henry. "Epitaph for Vietnam." *Washington Post* (May 7, 1981): p. F1.

"Architect Maya Lin Creates Her First Line of Furniture for Knoll." *Architectural Record* (June 1998): p. 192.

"Architect Attends Rite for Lewis and Clark Project." *Bismark Tribune* (May 2, 2005): p. 3.

Ayres, B. Drummond, Jr. "A Yale Senior, a Vietnam Memorial and a Few Ironies." *New York Times* (June 29, 1981): p. B5.

Baker, Dean. "Bridge to the Past." *Columbian* (Sept. 25, 2003): p. A1.

Baker, Dean. "Gateway to History; Architects Maya Lin, Johnpaul Jones Join Land Bridge Ceremony." *Columbian* (Nov. 18, 2005): p. A1.

Baker, Kenneth. "Carving Out Time." *San Francisco Chronicle* (Oct. 24, 2000): p. E1.

Block, Paula. "A Meeting of Minds." *Seattle Times* (June 12, 2005): p. 20.

Brake, Alan G. "The Boat in the Woods." *Architecture* (Oct. 2004): pp. 52–59.

Brettman, Allan. "Maya Lin Gets Hands-On." *The Oregonian* (Nov. 19, 2005): p. B1.

Brettman, Allan. "Maya Lin Sees Much More Than a Memorial." *The Oregonian* (May 1, 2005): p. B01.

Buckley, Christopher. "The Wall." *Esquire* (Sept. 1985): p. 66.

Cane, Mike. "Olympia Way Paved for Lewis and Clark Bicentennial Works." *Oregonian* (Jan. 24, 2002): p. B03.

Coleman, Jonathan. "First She Looks Inward." *Time* (Nov. 6, 1989): p. 90.

Eisen, Jack. "Commission Rejects Veteran's Protest, Reapproves Vietnam Memorial Design." *Washington Post* (Oct. 14, 1981): p. C3.

Farr, Sheila. "The Nature of Maya Lin." *Seattle Times* (April 16, 2006): p. K-1.

Fisher, Marla Jo. "An Exercise in Simplicity." *Orange County Register* (Oct. 26, 2005): cover.

Forgey, Benjamin. "Model of Simplicity: Another Look at the Vietnam Memorial." *Washington Post* (Nov. 14, 1981): p. C1.

Forgey, Benjamin. "The Statue and the Wall." *Washington Post* (Nov. 10, 1984): p. D1.

Frazier, Joseph B. "Where the Waters Meet." *Seattle Times* (Nov. 19, 2005): p. B4.

Goldberger, Paul. "Vietnam Memorial: Questions of Architecture." *New York Times* (Oct. 7, 1982): p. C25.

Goldberger, Paul. "Vietnam War Memorial to Capture Anguish of a Decade of Doubt." *New York Times* (June 6, 1981): p. 7.

Kastor, Elizabeth. "Maya Lin's Unwavering Vision." *Washington Post* (Feb. 13, 1989): p. B6.

Kirschenbaum, Jill. "Arts: The Symmetry of Maya Ying Lin." *Ms.* (Sept.–Oct., 1990): pp. 20–22.

Kramer, Carol. "The Wall: Monument to a Nation's Sacrifice." *McCall's* (June 1988): pp. 42–45.

Kreyling, Christine. "Lin Finds New Use for Old Barn at Langston Hughes Library." *Architectural Record* (May 2000): p. 48.

Lin, Maya. "Beauty and the Bank." *The New Republic* (Dec. 23, 1985): pp. 25–29.

"Maya Lin Dedicates Unprecedented Three Artworks to Mark Lewis and Clark Bicentennial." *PR Newswire* (Nov. 8, 2005).

"Maya Lin to Memorialize Lewis & Clark." *Seattle Times* (Feb. 19, 2001): p. B3.

McCombs, Phil. "Maya Lin and the Great Call of China." *Washington Post* (January 3, 1982): p. F1.

Menand, Louis. "The Reluctant Memorialist." *The New Yorker* (July 8, 2002): pp. 54–65.

Murphy, Jeremiah V. "Vietnam Scar Issue." *Boston Globe* (Jan. 23, 1982): p. 1.

Parfit, Michael. "Maya Lin." *Smithsonian* (Nov. 2005): p. 101.

Rowan, Victoria C. "Maya Lin Finds Inspiration in the Architect of Nature." *Architectural Record* (Sept. 1998): p. 56.

Rydzynski, Michael. "Q&A: 'This Feels Like Home Turf to Me.'" *Orange County Register* (Oct. 30, 2005): cover.

"Student Wins War Memorial Contest." *New York Times* (May 7, 1981): p. A20.

Swerdlow, Joel L. "Interview Maya Lin." *National Geographic* (May 1985), p. 554.

Tauber, Peter. "Monument Maker." *New York Times* (Feb. 24, 1991), p. A49.

Trausch, Susan. "U.S. Honors Vietnam Vets." *Boston Globe* (Nov. 14, 1982): p. 1.

Viladas, Pilar. "Mr. Norton's Cabinets of Wonder." *New York Times* (Feb. 21, 1999): p. SM56.

Washington, D.C., U.S. Federal News Service (April 25, 2005).

Von Eckardt, Wolf. "Of Heart and Mind." *Washington Post* (May 16, 1981): p. B1.

Wilkerson, Isabel. "'Art War' Erupts Over Vietnam Veterans Memorial." *Washington Post* (July 8, 1982): p. D3.

Wyatt, Edward. "In 9/11 Design, Rules Are Set to Be Broken." *New York Times* (April 29, 2003): p. B1.

DVDS

Lennon, Thomas, ser. prod., and Yang, Ruby, ser. ed.. *A Bill Moyers Special: Becoming American, The Chinese Experience.*

Maya Lin interview. Films for the Humanities & Sciences, 2003.

Mock, Freida Lee, and Terry Sanders. *Maya Lin: A Strong Clear Vision*. Docurama, American Film Foundation, 1994.

Sollins, Susan, exec. prod., and curator. *Art:21: Art in the Twenty-first Century*. Season One, Art:21. Distributed by Public Broadcasting Service, 2003.

WEB SITES

Academy of Achievement: A Museum of Living History. Available online. URL: http://www.achievement.org.

"Civil Rights Memorial," Southern Poverty Law Center. Available online. URL: http://www.splcenter.org/crm/memorial.jsp.

Confluence Project. Available online. URL: http://www.confluenceproject.org.

Destination: The Pacific, Lewis and Clark Bicentennial. Available online. URL: http://www.destinationthepacific.com.

"Future Memorial for World Trade Center Site: Reflecting Absence," Lower Manhattan Development Corporation. Available online. URL: http://www.wtcsitememorial.org.

Haley Farm. Available online. URL: http://www.haleyfarm.org/home.html.

"Maya Ying Lin's Latest Landscape Sculpture: 'The Wave Field,'" Francois-Xavier Bagnoud Foundation. Available online. URL: http://www.fxbfoundation.org/maya.htm.

Museum of Chinese in the Americas. Available online. URL: http://www.moca-nyc.org/MoCA/content.asp.

"Peace Chapel," Juniata College. Available online. URL: http://www.juniata.edu/tour/peace.html.

Vietnam Veterans Memorial. Available online URL: http://www.nps.gov/vive/home.htm.

Vietnam Veterans Memorial Fund. Available online. URL: http://www.vvmf.org.

Vietnam Veterans Memorial: The Wall—USA. Available online. URL: http://www.thewall-usa.com.

"Women's Table," Yale.edu. Available online. URL: http://www.yale.edu/opa/imagegallery/campus/source/23.html.

FURTHER READING

BOOKS

Ashabranner, Brent. *Always to Remember: The Story of the Vietnam Veterans Memorial*. New York: G.P. Putnam's Sons, 1988.

Lin, Maya. *Boundaries*. New York: Simon & Schuster, 2000.

Malone, Mary. *Maya Lin: Architect and Artist*. Springfield, N.J.: Enslow, 1995.

Scruggs, Jan C., and Swerdlow, Joel L. *To Heal a Nation: The Vietnam Veterans Memorial*. New York: Harper & Row, 1985.

DVDS

Lennon, Thomas, ser. prod., and Ruby Yang, ser. ed. *A Bill Moyers Special: Becoming American: The Chinese Experience*. Films for the Humanities & Sciences, 2003.

Mock, Freida Lee and Terry Sanders. *Maya Lin: A Strong Clear Vision*. Docurama, American Film Foundation, 1994.

WEB SITES

Academy of Achievement: A Museum of Living History. Available online. URL: http://www.achievement.org.

"Civil Rights Memorial," Southern Poverty Law Center. Available online. URL: http://www.splcenter.org/crm/memorial.jsp.

Confluence Project. Available online. URL: http://www.confluenceproject.org.

Destination: The Pacific, Lewis and Clark Bicentennial. Available online. URL: http://www.destinationthepacific.com.

"Future Memorial for World Trade Center Site: Reflecting Absence," Lower Manhattan Development Corporation. Available online. URL: http://www.wtcsitememorial.org.

Haley Farm. Available online. URL: http://www.haleyfarm.org/home.html.

Museum of Chinese in the Americas. Available online. URL:
    http://www.moca-nyc.org/MoCA/content.asp.

"Peace Chapel," Juniata College. Available online. URL: http://
    www.juniata.edu/tour/peace.html.

Vietnam Veterans Memorial. Available online URL: http://www.
    nps.gov/vive/home.htm.

Vietnam Veterans Memorial Fund. Available online. URL: http://
    www.vvmf.org.

Vietnam Veterans Memorial: The Wall-USA. Available online.
    URL: http://www.thewall-usa.com.

"Maya Ying Lin's Latest Landscape Sculpture: 'The Wave Field,'"
    Francois-Xavier Bagnoud Foundation. Available online. URL:
    http://www.fxbfoundation.org/maya.htm.

"Women's Table," Yale.edu. Available online. URL: http://www.
    yale.edu/opa/imagegallery/campus/source/23.html.

PHOTO CREDITS

INDEX

ABOUT
THE AUTHOR

TOM LASHNITS is a writer and editor specializing in history, biography, and the economy. For several years he worked as a researcher and writer at Time Inc., where among his many assignments, he contributed to books on art, photography, and film. He then moved to *Reader's Digest* magazine, and as an editor he developed feature articles and edited issues. Lashnits has written several Chelsea House books, most recently *Pedro Martinez* in the Great Hispanic Heritage series.